AF505430

ARTISTS ALL

ALSO BY BURTON RAFFEL

Criticism/History
   The Art of Translating Poetry
   The Development of Modern Indonesian Poetry
   The Forked Tongue: A Study of the Translation Process
   Why Re-Create?
   American Victorians: Explorations in Emotional History
   Politicians, Poets, and Con Men
   Robert Lowell
   T. S. Eliot
   Ezra Pound: The Prime Minister of Poetry
   Introduction to Poetry
   How to Read a Poem

Anthologies/Collections
   Poems
   The Signet Classic Book of American Stories
   The Signet Classic Book of Contemporary American Stories
   Forty-One Stories of O. Henry
   Possum and Ole Ez in the Public Eye: Contemporaries and Peers on T. S. Eliot and
      Ezra Pound

Translations
   Poems From the Old English
   Beowulf
   Sir Gawain and the Green Knight
   Chrétien de Troyes, Yvain
   Chairil Anwar: Selected Poems (with Nurdin Salam)
   The Complete Poetry and Prose of Chairil Anwar
   An Anthology of Modern Indonesian Poetry
   Ballads and Blues: Selected Poems of W. S. Rendra (with Harry Aveling)
   Gems of Chinese Poetry (with Zuxin Ding)
   From the Vietnamese: Ten Centuries of Poetry
   A Thousand Years of Vietnamese Poetry (with N. N. Bich and W. S. Merwin)
   Horace: Selected Odes, Epodes, Satires, and Epistles
   Horace: Ars Poetica (with James Hynd, David Armstrong, and W. R. Johnson)
   The Essential Horace
   Lyrics From the Greek
   The Bull Hide (La Pell de Brau)
   Russian Poetry Under the Tsars
   Selected Works of Nikolai S. Gumilev (with Alla Burago)
   Complete Poetry of Osip E. Mandelstam (with Alla Burago)
   Selected Poems of Alexander Pushkin (with Alla Burago)

Poetry
   Mia Poems
   Four Humours
   Changing the Angle of the Sun-Dial
   Grice
   Evenly Distributed Rubble
   Man as a Social Animal

Fiction
   Short Story 3 (with Robert Creeley and others)
   After Such Ignorance
   Founder's Fury (with Elizabeth Raffel)
   Founder's Fortune (with Elizabeth Raffel)

ARTISTS ALL

CREATIVITY,
THE UNIVERSITY,
AND THE WORLD

BURTON RAFFEL

THE PENNSYLVANIA STATE UNIVERSITY PRESS
UNIVERSITY PARK, PENNSYLVANIA

Library of Congress Cataloging-in-Publication Data

Raffel, Burton.
    Artists all : creativity, the university, and the world / Burton Raffel.
        p. cm.
    Includes bibliographical references and index.
    ISBN 0-271-00760-5
    1. Creative ability. 2. Creation (Literary, artistic, etc.)
3. Creative ability in science.   I. Title.
BF408.R14   1991
700'.1—dc20   90-20961
                                                              CIP

It is the policy of The Pennsylvania State University Press to use acid-free paper
for the first printing of all clothbound books. Publications on uncoated stock
satisfy the minimum requirements of American National Standard for
Information Sciences—Permanence of Paper for Printed Library Materials,
ANSI Z39.48—1984.

for my "best piece of poetrie"
Nathan Paul Raffel

Over and over, it seems to me, we are made aware in the history of thought of the primacy of the artist. . . . Not only is the artist likely to precede the scientist in recognition of the new or vital . . . but, in one and the same person, it is the art-element of consciousness that is likely to generate, through intuition and other states, best known to art, the elements we are prone to describe as scientific.
—Robert Nisbet, *Sociology as an Art Form* (1976)

. . . all mankind must follow the example of the artist, or, better yet, become artists themselves: for the word artist, *in its widest acceptation, means to me the* man who takes pleasure in what he does.
—*Rodin on Art* (1971)

CONTENTS

PREFACE

So much of my published work has been a kind of digging around in our collective past, trying to rediscover who and what we humans used to be, that I want to say at the start: This book is a synchronic, not a diachronic, quest. I know that in the larger scheme of things there neither is, nor can be, any set, permanent Western aesthetic, no fixed Western approach to creativity, just as I know there have been (and still are) other solutions to the social imperatives we try to satisfy with a vast, expensive, and at the moment increasingly unsatisfactory educational system. But my purpose here is to deal with the immediate situation, particularly as we confront it in ourselves and in higher education—or, more accurately perhaps, particularly as *I* confront it, for the pages that follow are surely a kind of credo. I like to think there is good reason behind this credo, and a lot of objective support, but I do not fool myself that I have discovered the vade mecum of creativity, or the philosophers' stone. I am certainly well aware that post-structuralist theorists have been attacking many of the cornerstones of this credo, casting doubt on the very existence of creativity (except perhaps in the books of literary critics?), not to say the existence of individuality, originality, authorship, artistic unity, and more. They have not convinced me; I suspect I will not convince them.

So I make no attempt, here, to account for how we got to be where we are or to distinguish what I take to be our operating rules from earlier belief structures. Our problems are neither inevitable nor unique—and I should like to hope they are not normative. We remain free to once again choose pathways once familiar but now long out of use: I do not consider negative social decisions any more permanent than positive ones. I have concerned myself almost exclusively with the here and now because the present is where we live and where, if we so choose, we are able to act. A Roman poet dead for two thousand years once said, in the words I put in his mouth: "Times goes running, even / As we talk. Take the present, the future's no one's affair" (Horace, *Odes* I, 11).

So too, although I have drawn on some non-Western materials, and remain passionately concerned with non-Western insights and modes for achieving them, this book is in no sense a systematic comparison of Occident and Orient. Again, there are waves upon waves of implications, as there are long and complex histories, lying behind issues that I may seem to treat with unbecoming casualness. I am in fact not in the least casual, but only urgently concerned, and determined at least to try to frame useful advice and workable solutions.

And not only do I too live in the present, but I am ever more pressingly aware that I live in it only transiently. At age sixty-two, with most of my days having been spent in higher education, I would like while I still can to offer some return on society's long investment. Among all my other far-flung obligations, lacing and interlacing through worlds and times, that is perhaps one I can partially repay. This book is therefore a conscious attempt to formulate whatever I have been able to learn about creativity and about our university world, after six decades of making mistakes, and to apply that knowledge to specific problems both individual and social. I am nobody's guru, not even my own. This is what I see; this is what I think about what I see; and these pages are what I have to say about what I think.

ACKNOWLEDGMENTS

Artists All began as a series of lectures, written for and delivered at the University of Southwestern Louisiana. I owe a large debt to Professor Doris Meriwether, head of the Department of English, who nominated me for the endowed chair in the humanities that I now hold; to Dean Richard C. Cusimano of the College of Arts, Humanities, and Behavioral Sciences for choosing to appoint me instead of the worthy candidates nominated by other departments; and to President Ray Authement, for the decision to award the first such prestigious and well-supported chair at USL—funded by a striking combination of state and private moneys—to the humanities. It was in recognition both of that fact and of the competitive, multidisciplinary environment from which the appointment came that I initially conceived *Artists All*, which was intended in the first place to say to all my new colleagues that I neither did nor could regard myself as representing the interests of any one academic department or discipline.

I owe a debt equally large to Dr. Sandra R. Wolman, who helped me begin to make sense of modern science, and to Professor Frederick Turner, whose dazzling *Natural Classicism* showed me what astonishing insights could be garnered with scientific tools. This book would quite simply have been impossible without their stimulus, suggestions, and friendship.

1

PERSPECTIVES
AND
GROUND RULES

The very word "interdisciplinary" seems to me a mis-nomer—almost, indeed, a contradiction in terms. To speak of a book or an essay as "interdisciplinary" is not just to assume the correctness of our ideas about intellectual "disciplines." It is also to assume that there are in truth meaningful boundaries between, say, physics, chemistry, and biology, or between English and French and German literature, and, furthermore, that crossing those boundaries is something like crossing an international border and passing from one fully independent nation to another.

Knowledge does of course have boundary lines, and I will be speaking about some of them. And certainly, in the many areas where disciplinary boundaries are either fuzzy, or shifting, or largely matters of academic convenience, it is not true that everyone is fully informed about everyone else's specialty. That is not true even inside any of the academic departments with which we currently operate. (It is also worth remembering that many of those departments would have been defined very differently fifty years ago, and others either did not exist or were viewed as mere subdivisions of some larger entity.) Not all physicists are up to date on the latest developments in Darwinian neurology; those who teach French do not necessarily know Goethe as well as do those who teach German. But there are basic assumptions, basic concerns, and a lot of important common knowledge as between, again, physics, chemistry, and biology or as between English, French, and German literature. And it is no more surprising to see scientists described as molecular biologists, or bio-physicists, or neuro-chemists, than it is to test literary theory by an examination of eighteenth-century translations, into French and German, of Samuel Richardson's English novel *Clarissa*, or than to conduct a study of poetics that deals with work in, say, Greek, Latin, English, German, and French.

There are large differences between the training received by scientists and literary critics, by musicians and psychologists. Of course: I am not suggesting orthodontal poetics, or biochemical counterpoint. Nor am I suggesting that all human beings are blessed with identical pitch sense, verbal acuity, or capacity for spatial and symbolic representation. There are good and sufficient reasons why Beethoven became a musician and not a geographer, and why Einstein became a physicist rather than a linguist. To think otherwise is plainly foolish.

On the other hand, there are greater similarities among all the branches of human knowledge than are usually recognized, and our failure to keep that fact well in mind can and does cause problems. One of the leading theoreticians of what became the study of fractals approached the subject from his area of professional concern, which happened to be weather prediction. He published startlingly important discoveries in the journals he himself knew and regularly read, namely, journals having to do with weather prediction. Scientists in other areas, not directly involved in weather prediction, were for a long time unaware of his discoveries, and their work was seriously hampered. Even when people work on the same campus, largely artificial departmental fences frequently—I almost said "usually"—keep us from being aware of what our colleagues are doing, to the detriment of each and all of us, and of course to the detriment of the pursuit of knowledge generally. Some practical steps have been taken—though nowhere near enough—to break through these barriers. For example, there are business and law schools using literary texts as teaching tools, and teachers of literature have always drawn on materials in music, visual art, and virtually all the social sciences. But these are bare beginnings, and as I say they are clearly not sufficient.

Let me illustrate how much there is to be learned, when we make it our business to follow along some of our neighbors' pathways, by citing the work of a distinguished mathematician, Henri Poincaré, whose 1902 study, *Science and Hypothesis*, remains one of the most powerfully useful investigations of the creative process ever set down on paper. Again, I will return to Poincaré on the subject of creativity later on: right now, I want to reinforce my comments about artificial and destructive disciplinary boundaries, a matter that Poincaré meets head-on:

> Let us first of all observe that every generalisation supposes in a certain measure a belief in the unity and simplicity of Nature. As far as the unity is concerned, there can be no difficulty. If the different parts of the universe were not as the organs of the same body, they would not re-act one upon the other; they would mutually ignore one another, and we in particular should know only one part. We need not, therefore, ask if Nature is one, but how she is one. (145)

Many voices have been heard, recently—including my own—arguing that our disciplinary divisions are both illusory and dangerous, and that until we realize the true oneness of intellectual inquiry we are going to continue to pay a severe price in sterile scholarship, dissipated energy, and ineffectual teaching. What I want to explore, in this book, is the essential oneness of that productive, imaginative self-mastery that I call, loosely, creativity, and the unified though apparently diverse ways in which creativity manifests itself in a variety of activities, literature above all, but also music, the natural and social sciences, and finally visual art.

But before I can begin to offer you such fruits as I am able to harvest, I am obliged to do some preliminary weeding and tilling.

In particular, I must take a very large step back and briefly consider the kind of stance from which we human beings tend to approach intellectual inquiry. How much of our intellectual activity is fully conscious? How much is less-than-conscious? (And note, please, that I do not say "unconscious.") Those staggering, much-beaten old horses, subjectivity and objectivity, are obviously still highly relevant. Again, Henri Poincaré has some wonderfully apt observations:

> It is often said that experiments should be made without preconceived ideas. That is impossible. Not only would it make every experiment fruitless, but even if we wished to do so, it could not be done. Every man has his own conception of the world, and this he cannot so easily lay aside. We must, for example, use language, and our language is necessarily steeped in preconceived ideas. Only they are unconscious preconceived ideas, which are a thousand times the most dangerous of all. (143)

We find it hard to admit that little of what we say or do all through our lives—not just when we are intellectualizing—is in the strict sense of the word "conscious." A more accurate description of our life process would be: "a journey conducted via automatic pilot." The opposite of "conscious" is of course "unconscious"—but the bulk of our lives is not led unconsciously so much as by rote and habit, by custom and rule. We sometimes say of ourselves, half laughing, that "life is what happens when you're planning something else." That is about as functional a definition as I know: we live according to what happens, not according to whatever we may have been consciously planning.

Nor are we usually as aware as we should be of the restrictive powers of language. We think of language acquisition as an unqualified good (though, as I will emphasize in more detail later, there is no such thing as an unqualified good: everything has its price, whether we care to acknowledge the fact or not). Certainly, one cannot operate effectively in human society—*any* human society—without having at least one language as a tool, and those who can wield more than one such tool are almost always at an advantage. But language also has its restrictive side, locking us into syntactical patterns that we have no choice but to accept, not often realizing how parochial the patterns of any individual language are apt to be. Most of us know, for example, that Oriental philosophies do not much concern themselves with direct cause and effect, nor with the kinds of precise details that occupy the attention of Western thinkers. But we are not usually aware that while the syntax of Western languages is detailed and precise, dividing speech communication into neat packages in which the subject agrees with the verb and the adjective is in the correct case, the syntax of Oriental languages is associative and combinatory, quite unconcerned with grammatical number, or gender, or even with such chronological matters as tense. If a speaker of Chinese or Japanese or Indonesian somehow wanted to be concerned with grammatical number, or gender, or tense, his language would fight him every step of the way, and inevitably defeat him. I once knew a lady who read Oriental philosophy, when she could, in French rather than English translation, because as between those two Western languages French is distinctly more friendly to conceptual matters, to generalization. But even French not only permits but actively encourages its users to count and to place situations in a reasonably exact chronological frame. These are things that simply cannot be done in Oriental languages: this is not the place to elaborate, for the elaboration would distract us from other issues I want to discuss, but the linguistic facts are clear. Even on the lexical—that is, the word-meaning—level, different languages deal with the world differently, and so must the users of those languages. It should not surprise us that Eskimos, for example, have many subtly varied ways of talking about snow and ice that are unavailable to us in English, or that in an indigenously nonscientific, nonclassificatory culture like that of Indonesia the language is not much concerned with the sort of distinctions about flora or fauna that have traditionally been so important to us. Every time I saw a magnificantly plumaged bird in Indonesia and asked what in God's name it was, I was given the same answer: *biru*, "bird." Every time I saw a new, incredible flower, larger and brighter than anything I knew existed, and tried to find out what it was I was seeing, I was told the same thing: *bunga*, "flower." As the linguist Edward Sapir nicely says:

> Human beings do not live in the objective world alone, nor alone in the world of social activity as ordinarily understood, but are very much at the mercy of the particular language which has become the medium of expression for their society. It is quite an illusion to imagine that one adjusts to reality essentially without the use of language and that language is merely an incidental means of solving specific problems of communication or reflection. The fact of the matter is that the "real world" is to a large extent built up on the language habits of the group. (162)

The psycholinguist Dan Slobin observes, after quoting this same comment, that "the striking differences between languages are not so much in what they are *able* to express, but in what they habitually do express . . ." (129).

But Benjamin Lee Whorf puts the matter most bluntly:

> In linguistic and mental phenomena, significant behavior . . . [is] ruled by a specific system of organization, a "geometry" of form principles characteristic of each language. This organization is imposed from outside the narrow circle of the personal consciousness, making of that consciousness a mere puppet whose linguistic maneuverings are held in unsensed and unbreakable bonds of pattern. (257)

Whorf beautifully applies this formulation to the consequences of English grammar:

> We are constantly reading into nature fictional acting entities, simply because our verbs must have substantives in front of them. We have to say "It flashed" or "A light flashed," setting up an actor, "it" or "light," to perform

> what we call an action, "to flash." Yet the flashing and the
> light are one and the same! (243)

Because we tend to live, in just this way, by patterns of which
we are rarely if ever conscious, we regard all our habitual ways of
acting and thinking (including of course our belief systems) as
natural and inevitable, even God-given.

Consider, as a small, practical example, the maxim, "The man
who regulates his life by principle alone is a monster." We may
smile and accept the warning, but for the most part we do not see
its powerful underlying truth. The maxim is plainly not sexist: its
reference to "man" clearly includes all human beings. We, all of
us, male and female alike, have a dangerous tendency to fall in
love with our own beliefs and rules.

But for the most part we never recognize, much less deal with,
what might be called the maxim's reverse side. The front side of
the maxim says that "man" needs to be careful because of his
built-in human limitations. But the reverse side declares, by necessary exclusion, that such extreme care is required precisely because, being man, we are *not* something else, higher and more
knowing beings who might safely formulate seamless, universal
principles of the sort denied to mere humans. For better or worse,
by being men we must acknowledge ourselves as finite, mortal,
intensely fallible creatures who cannot see around corners, cannot
comprehend how all things connect to all other things, cannot
perceive even the fragmented, limited nature of our perceptions.
And how should we presume?

But we do. We latch onto our finite, fallible rules and institutions with one hand, and with the other proclaim them universal
and eternally true. Nor do I mean "institutions" in any simple,
limited sense: all the pathways that we first tramp down, and
thereafter go walking along, are for us institutions. The mechanic
who squirms into the tightest of locations, always wearing his
denim hat, explaining that he would feel naked if he worked
bareheaded, has institutionalized hat wearing, just as surely as, in
the twentieth century, we have institutionalized the study of modern as well as ancient languages and literatures, or institutionalized
the study of science and deinstitutionalized the study of religion.
An American of a hundred and fifty years ago would barely

recognize what we today call a college curriculum; I do not think most such Americans, except perhaps for a very few like Thomas Jefferson, would much like what they saw.

We do not consciously recognize most of our institutions. We follow track lines we do not consciously know are there, obey signs we do not consciously need or bother to recognize. Confronted with someone who operates according to a different set of built-in (or automated) tracks and signals, we are therefore apt to be either dumbfounded or (even more likely) disbelieving and hostile. That is of course how it has always been: the word "uncouth," meaning slovenly and disgusting, comes from the Old English *cuthen*, meaning to be familiar with, to know. The man we did not know, the stranger, was automatically seen in a negative light: in Old English times, bluntly, the stranger was likely to be killed on sight. (And yes, there once was a word "couth," but it did not have anything to do with proper behavior. Chaucer, for example, speaks of "ferne halwes, couthe in sondry londes," meaning "distant shrines, known in various lands or places"; "uncouth" in the sense of something simply "unknown" is recorded as far back as King Alfred.)

Language is a form of culture—that is, man-made and man-perpetuated. Culture, to speak metaphorically, can also be seen as a kind of language. But what is more important is that our automated (that is, not-fully-conscious) procedures operate straight across the spectrum of human existence. I spoke about the meaning of the word "uncouth," but the very process of meaning itself is subject to powerful unconscious forces. One of the pathways familiar to every linguist is the attempt to create a change in language in order to effect a change in reality. We used to call the people who tend to airline passengers "stewardesses." They were uniformly female, young, and obviously chosen more for their physical attractiveness than for any other single quality, and most of us thought of them in what are now quite properly described as sexist ways. To help bring about a changed perception of what truly became a change in actual practice, the word descriptive of this occupation was altered to "flight attendant." And the change in language worked because the underlying reality had truly shifted. But the equally conscious attempt to deodorize the word "manure" by calling it "fertilizer," and later to deodorize "fertilizer" by calling it "plant food," worked only for a very short time, after which the unchanged underlying reality reasserted itself.

Much the same thing, though in more complex (not to say complicated) ways, happens with larger matters than mere words—with belief systems and institutions of all kinds. My father, who was a lawyer, used to refer to the proud boast of the Medes and Persians, who insisted that their laws never changed. And where, he would ask, are the Medes and Persians now? The power and strength of reality keeps asserting itself, whether we appreciate or even recognize the process. Institutions and belief systems *must* change to accommodate that reality if the people who live by them are to live successfully. No one truly knows just how these changes come about—but surely one explanation is that the people operating inside these belief systems and institutions change, thus forcing the larger structures also to change in order to accommodate (that is, to survive alongside) their patrons and clients.

Human existence requires institutions, and effectively functioning institutions require a high degree of predictable, habit-dictated behavior: there is no question about either the necessity or the desirability of such behavior. To a large extent, as all human beings have always done, we live as we must. A practical, functioning balance must be struck. Fully conscious existence, twenty-four hours a day, would surely be more than exhausting—it would be excruciatingly painful, and probably soon fatal. We need habit, as we need institutions and rules. But how much semiconscious regulation do we need, and how hard should we cling to what we have? What are the real issues involved in trying to gain more conscious control of our own existences? Lewis Carroll had a profound understanding of the terribly basic political issues such an attempt raises, either with respect to language or in terms of what that language describes and deals with:

> "But 'glory' doesn't mean 'a nice knock-down argument,' " Alice objected.
>
> "When *I* use a word," Humpty Dumpty said, in rather a scornful tone, "it means just what I choose it to mean—neither more nor less."
>
> "The question is," said Alice, "whether you can make words mean so many different things."

> "The question is," said Humpty Dumpty, "which is to
> be master—that's all."

In this book, I want to discuss that practical, functioning balance as it reaches across so-called disciplinary boundary lines. That is, in other terms, I want to discuss what I think of as high-order survivorship, which can be understood as just another definition of creativity. And creativity can be defined as a process of allocating time and energy so that the three stages of awareness I have been discussing—conscious and unconscious at the extremes, and habit or automated thinking and behaving between these extremes—all work together. The old-fashioned metaphor of the well-fitting, smoothly oiled parts of a machine is apt: friction between the parts of any organism is by definition counterproductive. And however we define those three stages of awareness, it seems plain that each stage must somehow be appropriately harnessed, yoked in a multilevel, harmonious functioning.

These are of course generalizations: until I have begun to fill in their outline, they necessarily lack content. I will begin to turn specific in just a moment. But let me first return to those constantly shifting, often distinctly illusory boundary lines we draw between disciplines. I believe passionately in discipline; I accept, though with distinctly reduced passion, the functional, practical, but essentially transitory utility of the academic conveniences we call disciplines—history, mathematics, political science, music, chemistry or biology or physics. But I do not believe such evanescent boundary-making lines go any deeper into the substance of reality than the chalk marks children scratch on city sidewalks. Like it or not, we are all in this together—this life, this exploration, this venture around, and in, and out, where we all circle and promenade from the moment we are born until the time we die: historians, mathematicians, political scientists, musicians, chemists, biologists and physicists—all of us. The basic tools we share, just as we share our common humanity, are the same—which is why I have entitled this book *Artists All*. As I will try to demonstrate, this is neither a romantic nor even a particularly glamorous notion. But just as the farmer must still separate wheat from chaff, no matter how rich and bountiful his harvest, so too we must constantly struggle to tell the ossified from the immortal, the rigid from the rigorous, the specialized from the truly special. If we are not as consciously hard on ourselves as we know how to be, day after self-critical day, it is virtually impossible not to quietly and steadily paint ourselves into corners, virtually impossible to be able to turn around and see the smooth surfaces of freshly applied paint behind which, stroke by stroke, we are becoming sealed.

Twenty years ago, when I lived in Buffalo, New York, my young stepson informed me that he did not want the sandbox I was preparing to build for him. Instead, he wanted a dirtbox: sand was too tame and effete—and, furthermore, sandboxes were too small. He wanted a truly big area, where his larger-than-life imaginings could take palpable form. He got what he wanted—and the first time it rained I discovered that his nine-by-twelve dirtbox was now a mudbox. He loved it, as did the other children in the neighborhood: washing machines, bathtubs, and other modern conveniences make the cleaning up of small children far less arduous than it used to be. I'm sorry to say that I started no trend: not only do I doubt the continued existence of that original dirtbox, but I strongly suspect there has never been a second one—at least, not one that had to be deliberately built.

But the concept has important validity for me. Not only do we regularly need to get our hands into the dirt, in order to preserve the basic life forces with which we operate, but we also need to lower ourselves from our prepared postures—our pedestals, if you will—and play like small children. Pablo Picasso once said that he had spent his entire life trying to learn how to draw with as unfettered and free a wrist as a child. Rather than semiconsciousness as a promoter of rule and regulation, he was referring to the truly unconscious as a kind of deep, spontaneous well from which he and all artists need to draw. When I taught at an art college, there was a student whose drawing had been virtually ruined by years of rule-inspired teaching. We tried, unsuccessfully, to get her to draw only when she was talking on the telephone—that is, only when her conscious mind was busy elsewhere and the ungoverned spontaneity of the unconscious could spring to the fore. Operating only with conscious or rote capacities, her work continued stiff, formalistic, drearily dull.

The true, deep unconscious is a relatively fragile resource: it will not usually stay available to us of its own accord, but needs to be cultivated and maintained. That is, we have to struggle constantly to keep the psychic channels open. I think of the late Woody Herman, coming to a recording date where, for the first time in his long career, he was supposed to function as a singer rather than an instrumentalist, but brought along his clarinet anyway. "Just in case the pipes get clogged," he explained nervously. The pipes do get clogged: we cannot ever forget that fact. Charles Darwin, faced with an early decision between and among science, poetry, and the life of religion, could not help choosing science. Almost sixty years later, with his life's work behind him and his career in science essentially closed, he records in the autobiography he wrote for his children and grandchildren that he tried to go back to poetry—and found he could not, for it was no longer there. Not only during the time of his *Beagle* voyage but for years afterward he "took much delight" in poetry; during the voyage, "when I could take only a single volume [on an excursion], I always chose Milton" (43). The shock and pain of the loss is obvious:

> Up to the age of thirty, or beyond it, poetry of many kinds . . . gave me great pleasure . . . I have also said that formerly pictures gave me considerable, and music very great delight. But now for many years I cannot endure to read a line of poetry: I have tried lately to read Shakespeare, and found it so intolerably dull that it nauseated me. I have also almost lost my taste for pictures or music. (73)

Darwin records that "this curious and lamentable loss of the higher aesthetic tastes" is both regrettable and, to him, incomprehensible. "My mind seems to have become a kind of machine for grinding general laws out of large collections of facts, but why this should have caused the atrophy of that part of the brain alone, on which the higher tastes depend, I cannot conceive." And he adds, self-deprecatingly, "A man with a mind more highly organized or better constituted than mine, would not, I suppose, have thus suffered." He also adds, significantly:

> If I had to live my life again, I would have made it a rule to read some poetry and listen to some music at least once

> every week; for perhaps the parts of my brain now atro-
> phied would thus have been kept active through use. The
> loss of these tastes is a loss of happiness, and may possibly
> be injurious to the intellect, and more probably to the
> moral character, by enfeebling the emotional part of our
> nature. (74)

Darwin's was a powerfully creative mind: that seems almost too obvious to need saying. To be sure, he had and still has his critics. But Loren Eisley was not in error when he declared, in a book so titled, that the nineteenth century was *Darwin's Century*. We should not be misled by Darwin's own modesty. He "was frequently to discover kingdoms while searching for asses," writes William Irvine, "and he was always cautiously following his nose to the most bizarre and extravagant destinations. His commonest reaction to experience was a well-bred ejaculation of amazement. . . . In short, Darwin muddled into genius and greatness like a true Englishman" (43–44).

But determined and wide-ranging as he was, Darwin remained a finite mortal, incapable of sustaining more than a certain span of active human concerns. It is no secret that, once out of our teens, we are able to remain intellectually active in a variety of directions, but that protracted interruptions in such activities result in sharply diminished capability and, before long, in loss of capability. Put more simply, people who go on into maturity still using their minds critically and in challenging ways can continue to do so—until, for any reason, they interrupt the process. Put more simply still, "use it or lose it." Claire and W. M. S. Russell, in *Human Behaviour*, explain this in evolutionary terms: "a human brain . . . as long as it remains progressive (i.e., forward-moving), will survive indefinitely, continually enriching its behaviour with new variability. . . . To explore is to survive" (23, 27). Jean Piaget phrases much the same conclusion with typically compact elegance: "we are tending more and more today to regard knowledge as a process more than as a state" (2). Darwin's loss of all ability to react to poetry, like similar losses for the rest of us, clearly reflects what happens when a potentially maintainable process is interrupted and stays interrupted long enough to become a discontinued process. At a certain point even the memory of the process is lost; the discontinuance becomes permanent; and what has been lost is lost forever.

These are genuine boundary lines: such deep and often uncrossable frontiers are as fundamental to human nature as man-made and transitory boundaries are trivial and transitory. When I was a high-school student, toward the close of World War II, it seemed likely that some of us might have to be navigators and bombardiers, so spherical trigonometry was added to the usual course in plane trigonometry. I managed very well with two-dimensional forms, in both trigonometry and geometry, but there is no force on earth strong enough to enable me to perceive and make sense out of great polar arcs and their like: I lack those capacities about as totally as, in matters musical, I lack perfect pitch. There are people who are in the very specific scientific sense idiots—that is, people with general intelligence in the very lowest measurable range— who can barely speak but who can sing rounds with deft perfection: I can sing rounds, imperfectly, only by covering my ears with my hands. But my poetic ear is in effortless tune, and for matters linguistic I have an instinctive *Sprachgefühl*: that sort of arbitrary but indisputable distribution of gifts and deficits is, as I say, human nature. Our intense divisibility, our abiding fragmentation, are realities against which the most determinedly egalitarian philosophy is utterly helpless. As an expensive, government-sponsored survey proved, some years ago, the basic reason that some schoolchildren get better grades than others is that some children are smarter than others. Smarter does not mean better or more important, but it does mean smarter.

But even if we do not know why a particular intellectual or emotional soil will grow brighter or more remarkable flowers, we can train ourselves to at least recognize the differences between and among those flowers, and then, if we are truly concerned, to understand that within certain boundary lines certain things are possible, while outside those same boundaries those things will not and cannot take place. Accordingly, just as Darwin could look back and declare, with profound regret, that if he had his life to lead over again he would take steps to ensure the survival of the capacity to relate to poetry and the other "higher aesthetic tastes," so too we can use these boundaries to recognize, encourage, and enlarge essential capacities over which we have only imperfect control. One of the central facts of the creative process, even arguably *the* central fact, is the maintenance of exactly this kind of responsive, reciprocal harmony between our conscious/outer and our unconscious/inner natures. This is neither a mystical nor a vague and sloppy, and certainly not a sentimental, assertion— and it is so central, indeed, that I must now take some time to try to elaborate and make concrete, practical sense of it.

Let me begin by reporting to you, with as little comment as possible, a few typical narratives of what it is like when the unconscious boils up and over and spills, like the Nile when it fertilizes Egypt, onto the conscious mind. And let me start, once again, with the French mathematician Henri Poincaré. In the essay "Mathematical Creation," he relates how, working with deter- mined intensity, he was unable to solve a problem until "one evening, contrary to custom, I drank black coffee and could not sleep. Ideas rose in crowds; I felt them collide until pairs inter- locked, . . . [and] by the next morning" the desired result had been attained. "I had only to write out the results, which took but a few hours." A subsequent illumination on the same subject came to him as he was stepping onto a bus. "I did not verify the idea; I should not have had time, as, upon taking my seat in the bus, I went on with a conversation already commenced, but I felt a perfect certainty" (Ghiselin, 36–37). And, as he later proved with what he describes as great (not to say almost casual) ease, he was right.

Poincaré goes on to explain, with considerable hesitation, that what he refers to as the unconscious or "subliminal" self has here worked through difficulties that the conscious self, unaided, could not solve. He is hesitant, clearly, because he does not fully under- stand the processes involved; his explanations are therefore, in his own words, "all very hypothetical." And yet he knows that

> such cases are frequent, and it is not necessary that the abnormal cerebral activity be caused by a physical excitant as in that [episode] I mentioned. It seems, in such cases, that one is present at his own unconscious work, made partially susceptible to the over-excited consciousness, yet without having changed its nature. (42)

Oddly, Poincaré's interpretation places more emphasis on hard work than on sudden illumination. Indeed, in his view "sudden illumination [is] a manifest sign of long, unconscious prior work" (38). There is of course a severe contradiction in this judgment, for only that which is conscious or perhaps, arguably, semiconscious can properly be called "work"; that which is "unconscious" simply cannot be thus labeled. He seeks to avoid the contradiction by saying that "this unconscious work . . . is possible, and of a certainty it is only fruitful, if it is on the one hand preceded and on the other hand followed by a period of conscious work." But the rest of his account reveals that even in his own experience these conditions were not met. He tells us that the bus episode occurred when he had gone on a "geologic excursion," and that "the changes of travel made me forget my mathematical work." That is, he had gone away from and even forgotten about mathematics, and indeed was occupied with other endeavors.

In fact, illumination of this sort is commonly experienced at unpredictable moments, neither preceded nor followed by any conscious activity. It usually comes while one is busy doing something utterly different, frequently something physical or extremely mundane—like stepping onto a bus. There is no directly causative, logically explainable sequence. I had put into print three different translations of the final line of an Indonesian poem, Chairil Anwar's "*Aku*" ("Me"), and was satisfied with none of them. The fourth and, as it turned out, final translation occurred to me as I was driving westward on the Long Island Expressway, not thinking about either poetry or Chairil Anwar. It was something of a shock, though a welcome one—a bit like suddenly seeing someone you hadn't expected to meet, or perhaps finding in a dusty, cheap bookstall a volume you'd been hunting unsuccessfully for twenty years. Sometimes illumination is insistent and unwelcome: the great Russian poet Osip Emilievitch Mandelstam spoke of a nascent poem as a nasty hum, or buzz, that tormented him until, finally, he consented to sit down and put it on paper. He would run out of the house, trying to escape, but never succeeded in getting away. To Mandelstam, as to me, illumination seemed to pop out of the air. To A. E. Housman, on the other hand, it seemed to burble up from the pit of his stomach:

> Having drunk a pint of beer at luncheon . . . I would go out for a walk of two or three hours. As I went along, thinking of nothing in particular, only looking at things around me and following the progress of the seasons, there would flow into my mind, with sudden and unaccountable emotion, sometimes a line or two of verse, sometimes a whole stanza at once. . . . Then there would usually be a lull of an hour or so, then perhaps the spring would bubble up again. I say bubble up, because, so far as I could make out, the source of the suggestions thus proffered to the brain was . . . the pit of the stomach. When I got home I wrote them down, leaving gaps, and hoping that further inspiration might be forthcoming another day. Sometimes it was, if I took my walks in a receptive and expectant frame of mind; but sometimes the poem had to be taken in hand and completed by the brain, which was apt to be a matter of trouble and anxiety, involving trial and disappointment, and sometimes ending in failure. (194–95)

But the capacity to draw on the unconscious is neither an unmitigated blessing nor an unconditional gift. Nothing is free; there are always trade-offs. To be prepared to listen to our deep unconscious voice means being unable always to listen to other, louder voices that speak to us in sometimes extremely important ways. It means resisting the siren call of the automatic, the habitual: what bubbles up from inside is never yesterday's printed menu, or the Boy Scout Code of Conduct. Trying to locate and hang on to the compass points of the "still center of the turning wheel," to borrow a phrase from T. S. Eliot, makes us less able to remember where the bank, the post office, and city hall are to be found. There are consequences to such practical inadequacies—which is one extremely important reason why artistic people, faced with a shortage of aristocratic and ecclesiastical patrons, have more and more turned to the universities. In the academic world, one is not usually expected to focus on the bank, the post office, or on city hall. That too, of course, has both its advantages and its disadvantages. Artists are grateful to their new patrons; in return, they usually dedicate themselves to their teaching and other duties with considerable zeal. But they also experience difficulties, for the academic world too can be narrow and the artist can come to feel stifled in its embrace. Nor does the kind of mildly monastic (though decidedly secular) life of the universities always seem as vital, as "real," as the life led outside campus walls. The painter Kenneth Evett, who was chairman of the art department at Cornell University when, in the middle 1970s, he made the remark I am about to quote, expressed both gratitude and discomfort with his academic affiliation: "The lack of connection with the real world and living at a level of privilege that is special compared to the way most people live means that you really don't have any idea of what real life is like after a number of years in this kind of environment" (*Artists as Professors*, 59–60).

The trade-offs can be a good deal more complex still. I say "can be," rather than "must be," because there are basic differences in the degree to which, in the practice of different professional lives, we may need to develop and draw on the unconscious. I think everyone with any kind of intellectual commitment needs some such reliance. But the practicing artist, whether in literature, music, or any of the visual or performing arts, requires a far deeper reliance, and therefore is also required to pay a much higher price to attain and to preserve it. It is not true that we cannot serve two masters: many of us do it all the time, and often we are not limited only to two. But it is profoundly true that adherence to more than one cause is apt to make us slight one or the other, or both. The artist in particular cannot make an easy or automatic adjustment to this basic division of loyalties, especially since his artistic needs drive him to turn away from precisely the kinds of engrained, rote activities that make for worldly comfort and success.

Again, let me be more specific. One of the hardest lessons for graduate students in creative writing is to learn that their chief enemy, their chief obstacle, their chief problem, is themselves. Asked for advice by someone who described himself as "a struggling writer," Isaac Bashevis Singer packed his response into two trenchant words: "Stop struggling." Learning how to work from within yourself, without worrying about what you will encounter, is painfully difficult. It is also crucially important. The difficulty can, I think, be summed up in one word: fear. Writers who have not yet found themselves, found their voices, found their subjects and their true stances, are usually writers who are afraid of what they will find. There is thus a special kind of vulnerability to the writer, as of course there is to all artists. In order to be open to themselves, in order not to be afraid of whatever boils and bubbles up from within, they have to keep themselves aware of and accessible to every kind of thought and emotion. To block anything may be to block everything, so it all has to be allowed. This is easy enough to say, but hard, and usually painful, to accomplish. No one can do it all the time; only the strongest can keep it up through all the long years of a full artistic life.

For musicians, too, and painters and sculptors, it is not the outer world that they must conquer, not the manifestations of craft and technique, but themselves. In every art, technique alone is sterile. In every art, any reasonably dedicated practitioner can fairly easily acquire all the technique that is needed. It is not the letter-perfect musician who thrills, nor the picture-perfect painter. Indeed, that sort of perfection is almost a sign of lesser artistic status: one of the things that makes Joyce Kilmer's famous and much-memorized "Trees" a bad poem is the absolutely perfect regularity of its metrics. I will say more about metrical regularity in chapter 4, but even a casual examination of what are clearly good poems written in traditional metrical patterns shows that irregularity is essential and invariable. If you can keep time with a spoon on a teacup as a poem is being read aloud, be sure what you are hearing is a bad poem. It used to be said of the pianist Artur Schnabel, a great interpreter who had a habit of dropping notes, that what he forgot to play was usually better than what most other pianists remembered. In the same way, no performing musician truly worth listening to plays the same phrase twice in the same way.

These are genuine boundary lines. There are of course others: I will try, as we go along, to enumerate as many as I can, and in specific contexts. But the whole issue of beauty and how we react to its presence or absence must be raised in this introductory chapter, for we tend to think of beauty as a limited phenomenon, of interest largely to such emotional people as—exactly!—artists. Nothing could be further from the truth. In Poincaré's account of mathematical creativity, for example, it is made completely clear that mathematical beauty is the key to the entire process: "This is a true esthetic feeling that all real mathematicians know, and surely it belongs to emotional sensibility" (40). Poincaré goes still further:

> Among the great numbers of combinations blindly formed by the subliminal self, almost all are without interest and without utility; but for just that reason they are without effect upon the esthetic sensibility. Consciousness will never know them; only certain ones are harmonious, and, consequently, at once useful and beautiful. They will . . . become conscious.

Just as mathematicians and physicists refer to an "elegant proof," so too almost all scientists speak of solutions that "satisfy," solutions that give back to their creators what they are searching for. It is axiomatic among scientists that as between two possible solutions, one of which is simple and elegant, the other of which is cluttered and complex, the simpler one is infinitely more likely to be true. Solving a problem is important; solving it well is equally important.

Jacob Bronowski phrases this somewhat differently, and as both poet and scientist his words have a singular authority:

> The need of the age gives its shape to scientific progress as a whole. But it is not the need of the age which gives the individual scientist his sense of pleasure and of adventure, and that excitement which keeps him working late into the night when all the useful typists have gone home at five o'clock. . . . All science is the search for unity in hidden likenesses. . . . The scientist looks for order in the appearances of nature by exploring such likenesses. . . . Science is nothing else than the search to discover unity in the wild variety of nature—or more exactly, in the variety of our experience. . . . What is a poetic image but the seizing and the exploration of a hidden likeness, in holding together two parts of a comparison which are to give depth each to the other? . . . Science, like art, is not a copy of nature but a re-creation of her. We re-make nature by the act of discovery, in the poem or in the theorem. (8–20, passim)

At the risk of excessive quotation, but in the interests of permitting those who have borne witness to speak for themselves, in their own words, let me bring forth one further testimonial, that of yet another mathematician, Marston Morse:

> The first essential bond between mathematics and the arts is found in the fact that discovery in mathematics is not a matter of logic. It is rather the result of mysterious powers which no one understands, and in which the unconscious recognition of beauty must play an important part. Out of an infinity of designs a mathematician chooses one pattern for beauty's sake, and pulls it down to the earth, no one knows how. (Nisbet, 5)

"There is never anything tidy, organized, or systematic in genuine discovery," as Nisbet himself emphasizes. "Art abhors all systems. So does the creative process generally" (15–16, 20).

Let me very briefly recapitulate. Like all human beings living in no matter what society, most of the time we deal with reality not like explorers in a strange land—which is for better or worse what we really are—but like aircraft making a nighttime landing at a giant metropolitan airport. We cannot see the night sky, we cannot truly see the ground, we know we are whirring blindly forward at incredible speeds—and somehow, using established procedures, and relying on artificial lights and radar and tracking beams and every other nonhuman resource we can, we usually make it safely down. I am acutely aware of what it is like to make such a landing with only human sensory apparatus as a guide. Coming out of the dark Adirondack Mountains and down into the small Lake Placid, New York, airport, which has no landing lights, no radar, no tracking beams, and which indeed is formally closed at dark, I frankly felt unmitigated terror. But the pilot knew his business, and knew his landing field, and we made as smooth and gentle a landing as I have ever experienced. There was in fact no significant danger—certainly no more danger than the automated return to land of larger aircraft at larger airfields. But reliance on our own senses can seem incredibly risky, and we naturally evade the opportunities, and avoid the possible consequences. Yet there are risks worth taking, and this kind of self-reliance seems to me one of them.

2
SOCIAL SCIENCE
AND
LITERATURE

When the Princeton psychologist Julian Jaynes investigated the origin of human consciousness in his fascinating study, *The Origin of Consciousness in the Breakdown of the Bicameral Mind*, he of course relied on literary evidence for much of the ancient period. "I propose," he declares, "to regard [the *Iliad*] as a psychological document of immense importance" (69). "Modern scholarship," he explains, "regards this revenge story of blood, sweat, and tears to have been developed by a tradition of bards . . . between about 1230 B.C. when, according to inferences from some recently found Hittite tablets, the events of the epic occurred and about 900 or 850 B.C., when it came to be written down." Reliable information about so ancient a time is plainly difficult to come by; Jaynes is hardly alone in drawing upon the *Iliad* as a source of nonliterary information. Eli Sagan's brilliant "psychoanalytic study of violence in ancient Greek culture," *The Lust to Annihilate*, would have been impossible without ancient literary texts. "All literature is a reflection of a system of values," writes Sagan; "great literature has the power to transform received values and thereby change culture. In the literature of the Greeks there was a pervasive interest in the forms of violence, and a continuing debate over the legitimacy of these forms" (4). These are but two, albeit two of the most excitingly productive, of such studies. All ancient literature is used, and rightly, to bear witness to every conceivable aspect of the time in which it was composed. The very language of such voices out of the grave is scoured for whatever clues we can wring from it.

Indeed, the literary view of such ancient texts as the *Iliad*, the *Odyssey*, and even the much more recent *Beowulf* (almost two millennia more recent), can be obscured by the determinedly archaeological approaches sometimes inflicted upon them. In 1936, for example, when Professor J. R. R. Tolkien—and he was a preeminent Old English scholar long before he became the world-famous creator of hobbits and the author of that splendid trilogy *The Lord of the Rings*—protested loud and clear against the overwhelmingly nonliterary view of *Beowulf*, the argument was still a hotly contested one and Tolkien was asserting revolutionary views. He argued so cogently that, today, he is rightly viewed as having virtually single-handedly brought about the truly literary examination of *Beowulf*. Tolkien's success may well have had something to do with his splendidly literary rhetoric:

> But it is plainly only in the consideration of *Beowulf* as a poem, with an inherent poetic significance, that any view or conviction can be reached or steadily held. For it is of their nature that the jabberwocks of historical and anti-quarian research burble in the tulgy wood of conjecture, flitting from one tum-tum tree to another. Noble animals, whose burbling is on occasion good to hear; but though their eyes of flame may sometimes prove searchlights, their range is short. (8)

The contest was so heated, indeed, and the nonliterary view held to so stubbornly, that when the distinguished scholar of all things

Japanese, Donald Keene, took his doctorate at the School of Oriental and African Studies, in England, after World War II, and for three years lived in the house and ate at the table of Professor Randolph Quirk, along with Quirk's graduate students in Old English studies, he came away with absolutely no idea that there *was* any Old English literature. Philology and archaeology were everything; literature was never so much as mentioned. (When earlier generations of Old English scholars did talk about *Beowulf* as a poem, they tended to speak with considerable condescension. Tolkien has some choice words on this topic, too, though I cannot stop to quote them.)

Literature has thus always been at least a passive influence on historical studies, as well as on investigations of ancient politics and political institutions and on a variety of anthropological and sociological inquiries. Just as there is social utility in the training function of the corpses dissected in medical schools, so too this passive role is a useful one, though somewhat limited. But the influence of literature can go a great deal deeper. As he was developing and shaping his theories, Sigmund Freud found strength in and at the same time struggled hard against literature's power. One of the case histories he contributed to his and Josef Breuer's 1895 volume, *Studies in Hysteria*, begins:

> I was not always a psychotherapist, but was trained in local and electrical diagnosis like other neuropathologists, and I still find it a very strange thing that the case histories I describe read like short stories and lack, so to speak, the serious imprint of science. I must console myself with the thought that it is obviously the nature of the material itself that is responsible for this rather than my own choice. In the study of hysteria local diagnosis and electrical reactions do not come into the picture, while an exhaustive account of mental processes, of the kind we are accustomed to having from imaginative writers, enables me, by the application of a few psychological formulas, to obtain a kind of insight into the origin of a hysteria. (*Origins*, 13)

Freud was later to come to terms with the potency of art's "fantasies," though even by 1930, when he wrote *Civilization and*

Its Discontents, he still clung to the conviction of the "higher" truths of science. By that time he could permit himself to recognize that "a great imaginative writer may permit himself to give expression—jokingly, at all events—to psychological truths that are severely proscribed" (57 n. 1). But he still felt compelled to at least try to keep art's power within "scientific" bounds, observing with an almost bland, blind faith that artistic creation "has a special quality which we shall certainly one day be able to characterize in metapsychological terms" (26). He also went out of his way to emphasize that the "pleasures and consolations" of "fantasy" are less durable and, though he does not explain how or why, less potent than the pleasures and consolations of what he chose to call "reality":

> People who are receptive to the influence of art cannot set too high a value on it as a source of pleasure and consolation in life. Nevertheless the mild narcosis induced in us by art can do no more than bring about a transient withdrawal from the pressure of vital needs, and it is not strong enough to make us forget real misery. (28)

Freud's ambivalence was never resolved. Immediately before the passage I have just quoted, he admits without reservation that "the substitutive satisfactions . . . offered by art are illusions in contrast with reality, but they are none the less psychically effective, thanks to the role which fantasy has assumed in mental life" (22).

And, as he had honestly but reluctantly admitted, thirty-five years earlier, he could not help himself. When Wilhelm Fliess, his early friend and collaborator, recommended to Freud that he read the fiction of Conrad Ferdinand Meyer, Freud not only accepted the suggestion but wrote, "I am reading C. F. Meyer with great pleasure," adding that "I shall soon send you a little essay on" one of Meyer's stories—in fact, the very first but certainly not the last application of his theories to works of literature (258). The "little essay" begins, significantly: "There is no doubt that this is a defence against the writer's memory of an affair with his sister. *The only remarkable thing is that this happens exactly as it does in neurosis*" (emphasis added). Freud adds, as if finding it hard to believe and almost as hard to face up to: "In every single feature it is identical with the revenge-and-exoneration romances which my hysterics compose about their mothers if they are boys." In the next paragraph, with the words following directly on those just quoted, Freud seems to switch subjects—but as he himself might have pointed out, the switch is more apparent than real, and the connectives are in fact quite obvious. He purports to have left off his analysis of Meyer's fiction and to now be discussing his own technical and "scientific" writing, probably a chapter of *The Interpretation of Dreams* and more than likely the analysis of a specific dream:

> The psychology is going curiously; it is nearly finished, was written as if in a dream, and certainly is not in a form fit for publication—or, as the style shows, intended for it. I feel very hesitant about it. All its themes come from the work on neurosis, not from that on dreams. (260)

The parallels with his immediately preceding literary discussion need no elaboration. And two weeks later, in sending the "scientific" work to Fliess, Freud is still extremely reluctant to have it read:

> Personal intimacy would have been an insufficient justification for letting you have it, but our intellectual honesty to each other required it. It was all written by the unconscious. . . . At the beginning of a paragraph I never knew where I should end up. It was not written to be read, of course—any attempt at style was abandoned after the first two pages. In spite of all that, I of course believe in the results. I have not the slightest idea yet what form the contents will now take. (261)

Again, the parallels with literary experience are too striking to need underlining. Two paragraphs further, Freud reveals that he is still voraciously reading Conrad Ferdinand Meyer's fiction, and getting large psychic rewards. "Our author's best novel . . . illustrates magnificently how in the process of fantasy formation in later years the imagination seizes on a new experience and projects it into the past, so that the new figures are a continuation of the old and provide patterns for them." He goes on at some length. Several months later, just after Meyer's death, Freud again significantly juxtaposes the difficulties he is experiencing with his technical work. Interestingly, he makes no formal separation, starts no separate paragraph, though he is usually punctilious about such formalities and in fact divides the short final section of the same letter into not one but two paragraphs. This time he implicitly fuses his obligatory reading in the "scientific" literature and the satisfactions he gets from reading Conrad Ferdinand Meyer's "fantasies":

> The literature on dreams which I am now reading is reducing me to idiocy. Reading is a terrible infliction imposed upon all who write. In the process everything of one's own drains away. I often cannot manage to remember what I have that is new, and yet it is all new. The reading stretches ahead interminably, so far as I can see at present. But enough of that. I marked the passing of our beloved C. F. Meyer by buying the volumes I lacked . . . I believe I am now as enthusiastic about him as you are. I can hardly tear myself away from his *Pescara*. I should like to know something about his life story and the order in which his books were written, which is indispensable for interpretation. (273)

The second part of this paragraph could easily have been written by a literary scholar. Plainly, Freud thus closely links the potency of his literary experience to the less glamorous but equally "necessary" reading in "scientific" work because, willy-nilly, he cannot bring himself to deny that potency. Later in his career, as we have seen, he did not bother to try, though he never overcame the discomfort of having to practice "science" with what he could not keep himself from labeling as "unscientific" tools.

Yet another example of much the same tension and struggle is Freud's uncomfortableness with the "unscientific" Jewish heritage into which, once again willy-nilly, he had been born. It must be remembered that even the most "progressive" among the Jews of Europe were only a generation or two out of the ghetto when Freud was born. Many Jewish communities fiercely resisted the dangerously Christian ideas of nineteenth-century Europe: the struggle to "modernize" took place in virtually all Jewish communities, but was most triumphant among those in German-speaking lands. For the Jews of Germany and Austria, in Freud's day and after, to be traditionally Jewish was emphatically not to be "modern," and science above all else was impeccably modern. To be traditionally Jewish, indeed, was to be virtually "medieval," to partake of darkly incoherent approaches that should somehow long since have been superseded. This tension was of course aggravated by the severe anti-Semitism of Austrian and German society, with which Freud also struggled all his life. But, as the psychologist David Bakan has shown in his study *Sigmund Freud and the Jewish Mystical Tradition*, Freud's views (and here I quote Bakan directly) are in many important ways closely parallel

> to the spirit of Jewish mysticism. . . . Somehow Freud had rewon and spoke from the vantage point of Kabbala and Jewish mysticism generally. . . . If he [was] conscious of the role of this tradition in his thought it would have been well for him to conceal such a fact in view of the intense anti-Semitism that surrounded him.
>
> It is essential to note, however, that Kabbala is only one ingredient in Freudian theory. Another element is the attitude of scientific analysis. Thus we may say of Freud that he subjected Kabbala to fine analysis. The yield may be conceived of as the integration of science and Kabbala, or the secularization and systemization of the intimate psychological features of Kabbala. . . . Just as Freud may be regarded as having infused Kabbala into science, so may he be regarded as having incorporated science into Kabbala. (298–99)

Nor, obviously, is Freud the only practitioner to employ literary materials for psychoanalytical purposes. The technique is universal. In his landmark study, *The Lonely Crowd*, the sociologist David Riesman first sketches the framework of his approach and then, getting down to brass tacks, explains that "it is perhaps the insatiable need for approval that differentiates people of the metropolitan, American middle class, whom we may regard as other-directed, from very similar types that have appeared in capital cities and among other classes in previous historical periods. . . ." And the proof?

> It can be argued, for example, that a copy of *The Spectator* [the literary journal put out by Addison and Steele] covered its potential readership more thoroughly in the late eighteenth century than *The New Yorker* covers its readership today. In eighteenth- and nineteeth-century English, French, and Russian novels . . . (22)

And we proceed at once to an intensive examination of Stepan Arkadyevitch Oblonsky, a major character in Tolstoy's *Anna Karenina*. Later in this same opening chapter there are references to the Homeric epics, to the Greek literary philosophers Plato (who began his career as a poet) and Aristotle, and to Aldous Huxley's novel *Brave New World*. Riesman of course uses other evidence as well. The point is, however, that he sees no essential difference between a citation to Tolstoy's fiction and a citation to Erik H. Erikson's work with the children on Sioux reservations. Both are equally good sources, equally reliable in their respective spheres.

The point becomes still clearer, I think, when we see how, in Karl Popper's massive *The Open Society and Its Enemies*, his discussion of Plato's philosopher-king seems to him not only properly concluded, but powerfully reinforced, by reference to a children's story, G. B. Stern's *Ugly Dachshund*. (The story was published in 1938, in which year, at age ten, I myself first read it; Popper was twenty-six years my senior, so he may have come across the book through his own children.) Raised among dachshunds, and thinking himself one, the protagonist is in fact a Great Dane, which stunning truth is only revealed to him, after wonderful misadventures, in the epiphanic and unforgettable ending. Popper writes:

> I think we must face the fact that behind the sovereignty of the philosopher king stands the quest for power. The beautiful portrait of the sovereign is a self-portrait. When we have recovered from the shock of this finding, we may look anew at the awe-inspiring portrait; and if we can

fortify ourselves with a small dose of Socrates' irony then we may cease to find it so terrifying. We may begin to discern its human, indeed, its only too human features. We may even begin to feel a little sorry for Plato who had to be satisfied with establishing the first professorship, instead of the first kingship, of philosophy; who could never realize his dream, the kingly Idea which he had formed after his own image. Fortified by our dose of irony, we may even find, in Plato's story, a melancholy resemblance to that innocent and unconscious little satire on Platonism, the story of the *Ugly Dachshund*, of Tono, the Great Dane, who forms his kingly idea of 'Great Dog' after his own image (but who happily finds in the end that he is Great Dog himself). (153)

In Daniel Bell's *Cultural Contradictions of Capitalism*, this fusion of social-science evidence and literary evidence is equally marked. "The bourgeois attitudes of calculation and methodical restraint," we are told,

> came into conflict with the impulsive searchings for sensation and excitement that one found in Romanticism, and which passed over into Modernism. The antagonism deepened as the organization of work and production became bureaucratized and individuals were reduced to roles, so that the norms of the workplace were increasingly at variance with the emphasis on self-exploration and self-gratification. The thread connecting Blake to Byron to Baudelaire—who is the avatar of Modernism—may not be literal, but it is a figurative symbolic lineage. (xxiv)

When "Blake and Byron and Baudelaire" have the same standing for an eminent social scientist as "the norms of the workplace" or "bourgeois attitudes of calculation and methodical restraint," there can be no doubt about the enormous importance as well as the complete acceptability of literary data.

And lest we be tempted to demur, murmuring perhaps that Daniel Bell is after all writing about cultural matters, and Karl Popper is an old-school man with an excessive fondness for sentimental parallels (and Plato is in any case too literary to count), let me cite Seymour Papert's *Mindstorms*, the subtitle of which is "Children, Computers, and Powerful Ideas." (Papert is professor of mathematics and education at M.I.T. and a specialist in artificial intelligence: no sentimental humanist he!) In the final chapter of *Mindstorms*, he discusses at considerable length Poincaré's ideas on the epistemology of the mathematical sciences. "Poincaré's [concept of the] unconscious," he points out, "is very different from Freud's. Far from being the site of prelogical, sexually charged, primary processes, it is rather like an emotionally neutral, supremely logical combinatoric machine." But Poincaré perfectly well understands, as Papert indicates, that "mathematical work does not proceed along the narrow logical path of truth to truth to truth, but bravely or gropingly follows deviations through the surrounding marshland of propositions which are neither simply and wholly true or simply and wholly false." Papert brings out Poincaré's belief in the essential role of the aesthetic sense and points out the utility of "showing how Poincaré's mathematical aesthetic sentinel could be reconciled with existing models of thinking to the enrichment of both." He discusses in some detail an experiment with nonmathematically trained people; he goes on to elaborate his own position at considerable length. And then he concludes this long discussion with the following:

> These remarks, although they remain at the surface of the phenomenon, suffice to cast serious doubt on Poincaré's reasons for believing that the faculty for mathematical aesthetics is inborn and independent of other components of the mind. They suggest too many ways in which factors of a kind Poincaré does not consider might, in principle, powerfully influence whether an individual finds mathematics beautiful or ugly and which kinds of mathematics he will particularly relish or revile. To see these factors a little more clearly, let us leave mathematics briefly to look at an example from a very sensitive work of fiction: Robert Pirsig's *Zen and the Art of Motorcycle Maintenance*.

After two pages of close textual analysis of Pirsig's fiction, Papert moves to another stage of argument, observing that "if styles of involvement with motorcycle maintenance are so intricately interwoven with our psychological and social identities, one would scarcely expect this to be less true about the varieties of involvements of individuals with mathematics" (194–205, passim).

Q.E.D.

Exactly this same full and easy acceptance of literary data appears in H. Stuart Hughes's study of "The Migration of Social Thought, 1930–1965" (the book's title is *The Sea Change*). At the end of a five-page analysis of Thomas Mann's novel *Doctor Faustus*, Hughes completely and unselfconsciously interpenetrates fiction, and the act of writing fiction, with the massive social changes he is documenting:

> Finally, in the narrator's constant asides to his readers, the novel reflected the tragedy of Germany in Hitler's grasp: beginning to write, as Mann himself did, when the bombardment of the Reich was mounting and eventual defeat was becoming a near-certainty, the imaginary Zeitblom [a character in the novel] finished his account nearly two years earlier than the actual author—at the supreme moment in the spring of 1945 when Allied tanks were rumbling unopposed through the countryside and the Second World War was crashing to its close. (249)

In Hughes's mind, clearly, there is no essential separation between and among novel, novelist, characters in the novel, and the stark physical realities of Nazi Germany and its grinding final defeat.

There is no point to multiplying examples: they are, as I have said, legion, and I doubt that further illustration could make the point any more clearly or forcefully. Objections that might conceivably be brought against any one of the examples I have cited simply cannot be brought against all of them: the conclusions I have drawn seem to me fully buttressed and unavoidable.

But let us look more closely, now, at the reasons for literature's so ready acceptance as primary source material for the social sciences. For ancient times, of course, unique availability is an obvious reason for such acceptance. For example, historians would love to have more information about the period after the departure from Great Britain of the Roman legions, ending with the migration to England of the Germanic tribes the Angles and the Saxons (England taking its modern name from the first-named of these tribes: *Angle-lond*, or "land of the Angles," a factual description that the earlier Celtic inhabitants, among them the mythical King Arthur, resisted as hard as they could). But almost all we know is contained in a literary-cum-historical book written in Latin by a seventh- and eighth-century Roman Catholic priest, the Venerable Abbot Bede. Right or wrong, complete or incomplete, Bede is inescapably *the* primary source, for there literally is nothing even remotely comparable.

But for the second half of the nineteeth century, is David Riesman obliged to turn to "English, French, and Russian novels?" Shouldn't a sociologist find more of direct relevance in the works of, say, so celebrated a fellow sociologist as Herbert Spencer? I have said that Freud could not help himself. Plainly, neither could Riesman, or Karl Popper, or Seymour Papert, or H. Stuart Hughes, none of whom exhibit the uncomfortable reluctance shown by Freud.

It seems to me that the answer is as basic, and at the same time as elusive, as a zen koan, those brief, trenchant narrations that are effortlessly illuminating, without seeming even to try. (*Ko-an* in Japanese, *kung-an* in Chinese, the terms means "official record" or "judicial case"; the koan has come to be a leading training tool in Zen Buddhism.) For example:

> In the Meiji period [late 19th century], a scholarly-minded Japanese went to Europe, where he studied in both Germany and France, took not one but two doctorates, and finally returned to Japan to teach Western philosophy. After some years, becoming aware that he had rather neglected his native traditions, he made an appointment with a Zen master, to see what he could learn. The Zen master received him graciously and, in traditional style, served tea. He filled the scholar's cup and kept on pouring, and pouring, and pouring, until finally the visitor cried out, "Enough! It's full!" The Zen master bowed. "So too," he said, "are you full of your Western knowledge. Until you pour some of it out, how will there be any room for Zen?"

I first came upon this koan, in very different form, in what still seems to me the best book on the subject, Paul Reps's *Zen Flesh, Zen Bones*. As a teacher, though to be sure not a teacher of Zen, I have been telling and retelling this koan for so many years that not only have I made it my own, I have also distinctly shifted its message, in addition to changing details to make them fit my changed presentation. D. T. Suzuki's explanation will do for me, too:

> The *koan* is neither a riddle nor a witty remark. It has a most definite objective, the arousing of doubt and pushing it to its furthest limits. A statement built upon a logical basis is approachable through its rationality; whatever doubt or difficulty we may have had about it dissolves itself by pursuing the natural current of ideas. . . . But the *koan* is an iron wall standing in the way. . . . Throwing your entire being against the *koan* unexpectedly opens up a hitherto unknown region of the mind. . . . Here lies the value of the Zen discipline, as it gives birth to the unshake-able conviction that there is something indeed going be-yond mere intellection. (108–9)

Absent the particular trappings of Zen Buddhism, the process Suzuki describes is essentially what happens when practitioners of social science make use of literary source materials. As we will see in the next chapter, the natural scientist too employs literary materials—but employs them differently. For what the social sci-entist understands, either implicitly or fully consciously (it does not matter which), is that he is dealing with deeply human situa-tions and that everything touched by human considerations is incompletely understandable by other humans. The rational, logi-cal approach will never, can never, reveal full truths. Indeed, to the extent that such truths can be perceived at all, it is only as integrated, experientially based wholes; they cannot be formulated or expressed in rational, logical terms. Or, to rephrase this conclu-sion in strictly literary terms: while expository prose, which is carefully based on orderly syntactical arrangements, is capable of clear statements about linear events, literary prose and, especially, poetry do a good deal better with nonlinear occasions. Or, to rephrase yet again, returning for a moment to Zen terminology: when a Zen master is congratulated on knowing the true meaning of a doctrine, he very properly answers, "How could this doctrine have any 'meaning'?" If he is then asked, "How can there be understanding if there is no meaning?" the Zen master will reply, conclusively, "To understand a doctrine is not to know its meaning." Just as there is a world of difference between "understanding" something and knowing its "meaning," so too there is a vast gulf between understanding a human situation and laying out a reasoned, rational proof of that understanding. A koan can help bring about understanding; a koan has nothing whatever to do with proof. So too analyses of poetry and fiction, like anecdotal narration or dramatic re-creation, can help us understand, without fixing that understanding in any kind of proof. To his credit, the good practitioner of social science is usually well aware both of what he can and of what he cannot do. But the social scientist who thinks that human problems, like mathematical or physical ones, can be dealt with through logic and proofs can get into quagmires of wasted effort and ultimately rather foolish failures of comprehension. A well-known political scientist once explained to me how, using elaborately "scientific" charts and tables, he could predict the votes of Supreme Court justices with an accuracy rate approaching 70 percent. I assured him that, without any tables or charts, any good lawyer who followed the Court could predict those same votes with an accuracy rate closer to 85 or even 90 percent.

The closest linkage between any of the social sciences and literature is of course reserved for historical studies. It is no accident that a good many historians have also been writers of novels, and that a good many writers of novels—myself included—have also written historical studies. I am of course hardly the first to deal with the manifold interconnections between literature and history. In 1947, for example, Emery Neff published a study, *The Poetry of History*, which was subtitled "The Contribution of Literature and Literary Scholarship to the Writing of History Since Voltaire." Neff explains that he "might [equally well] have named [his book] 'The Artistry of Knowledge,' to describe the means historians have chosen to win humanity to recognize its own likeness, to understand itself" (4). He dedicates the book "To those who believe that knowledge is one and indivisible."

Although I do not believe that knowledge is in fact either unitary or indivisible, Neff's goals and mine are in most respects similar. In his words, his aim is the "breaking down [of] the compartments of literature, history, science, social studies and philosophy, to exhibit the interdependence of ideas, events, and art" (vii). Neff and I would both agree with the late, great Carl Becker, who was also actively concerned with the best way to make history fulfill its own programs. Becker declared bluntly that "in truth the actual past is gone; and the world of history is an intangible world, re-created imaginatively, and present in our minds" (52). Accordingly, just as Freud *had* to turn to imaginative re-creations, to trace out much of what he was learning about the human psyche, so too, and in still more basic ways, must all historians. "By no possibility," Becker explains, "can the historian present in its entirety any actual event, even the simplest." "History as something experienced can never be fully recorded," in Aldous Huxley's words. "For, obviously, there are as many such histories as there have been experiencing human beings. . . . History-as-something-experienced being unwritable, we must perforce be content with history-as-something-in-the-minds-of-historians" (222–23). But "let us guard against stripping [history] of its share of poetry," warned Marc Bloch in 1942, in the never-completed manuscript *The Historian's Craft*, at which he worked while he and others in the French Resistance continued their fight against Nazi Germany in which, two years later, Bloch met his death. "Let us also beware," he urged, "of the inclination, which I have detected in some, to be ashamed of this poetic quality. It would be sheer folly to suppose that history, because it appeals strongly to the emotions, is less capable of satisfying the intellect" (8).

"But if history in the objective sense is not *all* that has happened," asks James T. Shotwell, "*how much* is it of what has happened?" Shotwell, writing in the late 1930s, complained that "history has generally been regarded as a branch of literature. Historians have been treated as masters of style or of creative imagination, to be ranked alongside poets or dramatists, rather than simply as historians . . ." (7, 3). But is the complaint justified? History does not and of course can not concern itself with *all* that has happened, as Shotwell realizes. But everything history does record as happening should actually have happened, and pretty much as the historian records it. If scholarship in no matter what field is to mean anything, there must be strict fidelity to the truth. Yet what is historical "truth"? It is the rare historian who has actually seen, actually participated in the events he describes and analyzes. Not that firsthand evidence must necessarily come from the historian himself. There are good firsthand sources for many historical epochs, and especially for such notable events as battles, marriages, love affairs, and all manner of assorted catastrophes. What we usually mean by a "historical fact," indeed, is something that can be verified, either by some reliable document or by the reliable testimony of one or more individuals, either participants or firsthand observers or else persons verifiably knowledgeable and more likely to be truthful than otherwise. When we read that Thomas Stearns Eliot was born in 1888 in St. Louis, Missouri, and educated at Harvard, the Sorbonne, and Merton College, Oxford, we expect that there is a birth certificate, or its equivalent, to substantiate the first "fact" and various other documents to verify the others. And indeed for T. S. Eliot's birth, and for much of his life, there are documents aplenty. Yet it is still for the historian to reimagine those events—and as Carl Becker insists,

> our imagined picture of the actual event is always deter-mined by two things: (1) by the actual event itself insofar as we can know something about it; and (2) by our own present purposes, desires, prepossessions, and prejudices, all of which enter into the process of knowing it. . . . The historian cannot eliminate the personal equation. . . . The physicist can eliminate the personal equation to a greater extent, or at least in a different way, than the historian, because he deals, as the historian does not, with an exter-nal world directly. The physicist presides at the living event, the historian presides only at the inquest of its remains. (57, 56)

John Higham's *Reconstruction of American History* gives us a still broader perspective. "The writing of American history has always had . . . an intimate relation to history in the making. To examine the two together is to see America in terms of its evolving consciousness of itself" (10). Frances FitzGerald has recently studied exactly this phenomenon, in the specific context of the history texts we use in our lower schools. Her report, *America Revised*, is chillingly written:

> To read the texts published over the two hundred years of United States history is to see several complete revisions in the picture they present of the country and its place in the world. These apparently solid, authoritative tomes are in fact the most nervous of objects, constantly changing in style as well as in political content. (47)

But FitzGerald is surely somewhat naïve. She is of course absolutely correct about the character and quality of the texts she analyzes. They are indeed pretty poor objects, and those of us who work in other vineyards than history must usually say the same thing about the lower-school texts in our fields; for some subject areas, I'm afraid I would myself have to include university texts as well, for the homogenization and group-think processes have afflicted and damaged us all. But the intensely subjective aspect of historical writing makes it inevitable that there be quite as many visions and revisions as we find in any of the avowedly subjective arts. These are not simply stylistic shifts, but changes in perspective and approach that embrace, also, changes in major historical values, even changes in how we see the "facts" from which we construct each new set of historical "truths." Sidney Eisenstadt explains:

> Each age has its new history. In each new history, further vistas are opened up, while, no less significantly, several are closed. New experiences alter a society and alter too its perspectives on the past, demanding new insights for new relevances and making many old insights irrelevant. No age has been without its historical renovation, and no new history has claimed anything less than a wish to renovate the whole past and nothing but the whole past. (vol. 2, 1)

All we would need to do, to make this comment applicable to literature, or music, or art, would be to substitute "literature" or "music" or "art" for "history." Nothing else is required; the fit is perfect.

George Kennan has recorded that, when he left government service and became a practicing historian, the discovery of the "artistic" side of the discipline totally dismayed him. (We have of course seen that dismay before: Sigmund Freud is in very good company.) Kennan was upset at "the hopeless open-mindedness" of history, "its multi-dimensional quality, its lack of tidy beginnings and endings, its stubborn refusal to be packaged in any neat and satisfying manner." He was dismayed, too, "to discover how rigorous . . . were the limitations of perspective." History could not be seen "from all directions at once." You had to pick your point of observation, which was "always arbitrary in relation to the subject," but once you had chosen it you remained aware not only that "an infinite number of other points could conceivably have been selected" but, almost more depressing, that the built-in subjectivity of the whole process raised "a real question as to what latitude you really had in selecting the point you were going to use—whether, in fact, it was not already substantially selected for you." And what *this* meant, Kennan discovered, was "that the fixed point from which one viewed history was actually none other than one's own self—one's self in the most intimate personal sense." And what this in its turn meant, finally, was that "the describing of historical events . . . was partly an act of the creative imagination of the writer" ("The Experience of Writing History," in Eisenstadt, vol. 2, 270–72).

There remain historians, of course, who try manfully to reject all such notions. J. H. Plumb, for example, insistently compares history to natural science, and quite scornfully disclaims connections to such utterly different disciplines as literature, classical studies, or even the social sciences. To him, history is professional, scientific, objective, and—of course—unique. And yet, in a chapter entitled "The Role of History" in his book *The Death of the Past*, Plumb makes some revealing admissions—unconsciously, I think, but very clearly. He explicitly calls Marc Bloch "the greatest historian of modern times," a judgment that is certainly defensible, and then explains his evaluation as follows. Note carefully the almost stunning contradictions between the two halves of this explanation, beginning with the bland disclaimer "and yet":

> Bloch combined two qualities. He possessed the power to abstract himself from any preconceived notions about the past and to investigate an historical problem with detachment. And yet, detached as he was, his imagination, his creative invention, his sense of humanity infused all that he did. (85–86)

Plumb makes it plain that he has not the slightest interest in

> a philosophic discussion of the nature of history or of its capacity to establish objective truth. The practising historian is like the practising scientist. Just as the latter has no great interest in or use for the philosophy of science, so the active historian is not much concerned with the philosophy of history. He knows history exists and he has been trained in the necessary methods for its investigation. (84)

Yet Plumb's own language carefully sets off the "imagination" of the historian against the supposed "detachment" he so cherishes. More: the very syntax by which he structures his statement links "creative invention" to "imagination," and then links it to yet a third equally "subjective" element, the historian's "humanity." Indeed, can the imagination or a person's creative invention work *without* those "preconceived notions" that Plumb overtly condemns? And what does it mean to claim for someone a "sense of humanity," if not to ascribe to him warmth and compassion and generosity and the like—all qualities of an inherently, unavoidably subjective nature and effect?

And the contradiction becomes still more basic, for Plumb concludes both his chapter and his book by arguing that "the one truth of history" is

> that the condition of mankind has improved, . . . and it is the duty of the historian to teach this, to proclaim it, to demonstrate it in order to give humanity some confidence in a task that will still be cruel and long—the resolution of

the tensions and antipathies that exist within the human species. (113)

It would be hard to construct a less detached, a more subjective program: the high moral tone cannot conceal how Plumb fairly wallows in self-approval of his personal goals, his personal ideals, his personal righteousness.

Let me conclude by briefly turning to this matter of the deceptive and self-deceptive power and use of language. There is no need to do more, I think, than set out the brilliant analyses written many years ago by Aldous Huxley and George Orwell, superbly professional writers who had more than enough experience of the rhetorical sins they describe. These analyses have deeply influenced my own thinking; I want to quote them at some length, because I do not think I can improve on them. Here, first, is Huxley:

> Consider, for example, the case of war. . . . To developed sensibilities the facts of war are revolting and horrifying. . . . Now, language is, among other things, a device which men use for suppressing and distorting the truth. Finding the reality of war too unpleasant to contemplate, we create a verbal alternative to that reality, parallel with it, but in quality quite different from it. That which we contemplate thenceforward is not that to which we react emotionally . . . , is not war as it is in fact, but the fiction of war. . . . The language of strategy and politics is designed, so far as it is possible, . . . to make it appear as though wars were not fought by individuals drilled to murder one another in cold blood and without provocation, but either by impersonal and therefore wholly non-moral and impossible forces, or else by personified abstractions. . . . In place of "cavalrymen" or "foot-soldiers" military writers like to speak of "sabres" and "rifles." Here is a sentence from a description of the Battle of Marengo: "according to Victor's report, the French retreat was orderly; it is certain, at any rate, that the regiments held together, for the six thousand Austrian sabres found no opportunity to charge home." The battle is between sabres in line and muskets in echelon—a mere clash of ironmongery.

Alternatively the combatants are personal, in the sense that they are personifications. There is "the enemy," in the singular, making "his" plans, striking "his" blows. . . . And how reassuring is the language of historians and strategists! They write admiringly of those military geniuses who know "when to strike at the enemy's line"; . . . when to "turn his flank"; when to "execute an enveloping movement." As though they were engineers discussing the strength of materials and the distribution of stresses, they talk of abstract entities called "man power" and "fire power." They sum up the long-drawn sufferings and atrocities of trench warfare in the phrase, "a war of attrition"; the massacre and mangling of human beings is assimilated to the grinding of a lens. (246–48)

Orwell makes much the same argument:

In our time, political speech and writing are largely the defence of the indefensible. . . . Political language has to consist largely of euphemisms, question-begging and sheer cloudy vagueness. Defenceless villages are bombarded from the air, the inhabitants driven out into the countryside, the cattle machine-gunned, the huts set on fire with incendiary bullets: this is called *pacification*. Millions of peasants are robbed of their farms and sent trudging along the roads with no more than they can carry: this is called *transfer of population* or *rectification of frontiers*. People are imprisoned for years without trial, or shot in the back of the neck or sent to die of scurvy in Arctic lumber camps: this is called *elimination of undesirable elements*. (153)

Huxley's conclusions seem to me impossible to evade: "Reality," he declares, "is a succession of concrete and particular situations. When we think about such situations we should use the particular and concrete words which apply to them. If we use abstract words which apply equally well (and equally badly) to other, quite dissimilar situations, it is certain that we shall think incorrectly" (249).

My own conclusion is that if we try to use clear and concrete language, and try to be aware of our own fallibilities and limitations as merely mortal beings, and recognize that those same human limitations also contain the possibilities for creative exploitation—for cheerfully operating as much like the inevitably subjective, emotion-ridden men and women we in fact are—then we have a reasonable chance of producing good, useful work that will be genuinely meaningful to other fallible, mortal beings exactly like ourselves. Neither scholarship nor the pursuit of the highest of abstract goals can remove us from our fundamental, ineluctable humanity. Why not, as Tantric Buddhism so sensibly urges, ride on our limitations, instead of having them ride on us?

3
NATURAL SCIENCE AND LITERATURE

Science has powerfully affected every aspect of the modern world; literature is only one tributary through which this pervasive influence has flowed. Indeed, before discussing some of the linkages between the practice of science and the practice of literature, let me begin with our current view of the brain and how that soft, skull-bound, indispensable organ interconnects thought and emotion, for the ways in which we *think* we think shape both how we actually do think and the kinds of things we think about. As Albert Einstein observed,

> The whole of science is nothing more than a refinement of everyday thinking. It is for this reason that the critical thinking of the physicist cannot possibly be restricted to the examination of concepts in his own specific field. He cannot proceed without considering critically a much

more difficult problem, the problem of analyzing the nature of everyday thinking. (Miller, *Imagery*, 13)

A quarter of a century ago, when I was teaching a basic course
in linguistics, I regularly invited a physiological psychologist who
was deeply involved in brain research to lecture to my class. After
his first appearance I asked him, with some surprise, "Is that all?
Is that really the sum of what you know about how the brain
functions? Are your theories no more complex or sophisticated
than that?" He smiled and answered "yes" to all my questions. In
his 1987 *Neural Darwinism*, subtitled "The Theory of Neuronal
Group Selection," the Nobel Prize–winning biologist Gerald M.
Edelman, director of the Neurosciences Institute at Rockefeller
University, is still confronting great abysses of uncertainty:

> A theory about complex systems necessarily has to contain
> a number of partial theories and models. . . . In view of the
> intricacies of neural function, the likelihood is great that
> certain mechanistic details in the models subsumed under
> the main theory will turn out to be incorrect. . . . [Indeed,]
> formulation of the theory of neuronal group selection . . .
> has required a rather severe restriction of the domains of
> higher brain function to be considered. . . . [And] until the
> restricted form of the theory is tested . . . , it will be almost
> fruitless to attempt a consideration of the basis in brain
> function of higher-level concepts, thinking, or other related
> cognitive matters. Above all, the issue of language remains
> to be addressed along with notions of self-consciousness
> and awareness that lead to perceptual experience. (315,
> 328)

In the past twenty-five years, there has been a great deal of brain
research, both psychological and biological, and much interesting,
sometimes fruitful theorizing. We have new and tantalizing clues,
whiffs of understanding, glimmers of what we hope and believe
are further steps along the road to comprehension. But in many if
not most respects we are not much further down that road than
was Mr. Ramsay, in Virginia Woolf's *To the Lighthouse*:

> If thought is like the keyboard of a piano, divided into so
> many notes, or like the alphabet is ranged in twenty-six
> letters all in order, then his splendid mind had no sort of
> difficulty in running over those letters one by one, firmly
> and accurately, until it had reached, say, the letter Q. . . .
> But after Q? What comes next? After Q there are a number
> of letters the last of which is scarcely visible to mortal eyes,
> but glimmers red in the distance. . . . Still, if only he could
> reach R it would be something. . . . [But] a shutter, like the
> leathern eye of a lizard, flickered over the intensity of his
> gaze and obscured the letter R. (35–36)

Mr. Ramsay is modeled on Virginia Woolf's father, Leslie Stephen, and in this passage she is quietly mocking him, at the same time as she is also admiring his persistence in inquiry. But mankind as a whole has not reached anywhere near as far as "Q." That same leathern shutter still hangs right over our dim, squinting eyes.

As recently as 1980, for example, Edward O. Wilson could state authoritatively, but not fully knowledgeably, that "self-knowledge is constrained and shaped by the emotional control centers in the hypothalamus and limbic system of the brain. These centers flood our consciousness with all the emotions—hate, love, guilt, fear, and others . . ." (3). But more recent work by Joseph LeDoux has shown that there is a specific part of the brain, the amygdala, that operates completely independently of all the cortical functions, receiving and storing emotions and later acting on the basis of those emotions without any reference to or control by our rational, conscious mind. This pre-cognitive functioning explains, for the first time, why virtually everything we feel and experience in the first several years of life remains consciously inaccessible to us, though no one doubts that it has vast influence on our lives (*New York Times*, 15 August 1989, 15, 19).

Perhaps the first and even the primary point at which science and literature intersect is their mutual concern with the nonlinear. Poets in particular have always known that their art is centered in investigations of important affective processes that are largely inaccessible to more straightforward linear probing. The history of prose fiction in the twentieth century might well be written, some day, in terms of how novelists explored exactly these same domains of the nonlinear. But scientists too are increasingly and articulately aware of how pervasive nonlinearity is in their work. Scientists have always been aware of the nonlinear, even if only in a negative sense. In the thought of ancient Greece "the concept of the infinite," writes Morris Kline,

> is scarcely understood and frankly avoided. The simplest type of motion for the Greeks is not, as it is for us, along a straight line, because the straight line is not perceptible in its entirety: straight-line motion is never completed. The Greeks preferred circular motion. The concept of a limitless process frightened them. . . . (57)

All through the nineteeth century, and well into the twentieth, we struggled to preserve the relatively straightforward cause-and-effect theory of Newtonian science, which beautifully fits our determined, lingering insistence on an ordered, regulated world. James Gleick, in his brilliant 1987 popularization, *Chaos*, explores and summarizes the growing understanding among scientists that the universe as it exists both outside and inside us has deeply nonlinear characteristics. As he notes, "small nonlinearities were easy to disregard. People who conduct experiments [i.e., scientists] learn quickly that they live in an imperfect world. In the centuries since Galileo and Newton, the search for regularity in experiment has been fundamental" (41). Accordingly, still quoting Gleick, "the shapes of classical geometry are lines and planes, circles and spheres, triangles and cones. They represent a powerful abstraction of reality, and they inspired a powerful philosophy of Platonic harmony." But

> clouds are not spheres, [and] . . . mountains are not cones. Lightning does not travel in a straight line. The new geometry mirrors a universe that is rough, not rounded. . . . It is a geometry of the pitted, pocked, and broken up, the twisted, tangled, and intertwined. . . . [And] the pits and tangles are more than blemishes. . . . They are often the keys to the essence of a thing. (94)

Accordingly, what the new geometry has had to recognize, just as, significantly, the new music and the new art and the new literature have long since recognized, is that "the world displays a regular irregularity" (98). The basic mathematical shapes of this new geometry are called fractals. And as Gleick explains, "often the scientists drawn to fractal geometry felt emotional parallels between their new mathematical aesthetic and changes in the arts in the second half of the [twentieth] century. They felt that they were drawing some inner enthusiasm from the culture at large" (116). It has been my argument, throughout, that that is not only exactly what they were doing, but that the whole process is inevitable, unavoidable. The impulses that drive one aspect of culture drive all aspects. "Pattern born amid formlessness," says Gleick, "is biology's basic beauty and its basic mystery." Gerald Edelman observes: "The environment or niche to which an organism must adapt is not arranged according to logic, nor does it have absolute values assigned to its possible orderings" (24). The arguments are strictly parallel, though Gleick is arguing principally from mathematics and physics and Edelman is working with biology. But the very newness and originality, as well as the profundity, of Edelman's "neural Darwinism" is precisely that he has disdained the search for preprogrammed, fully ordered neural development and is arguing powerfully and persuasively that the individual brain, if it does not quite tumble into existence like Topsy, nevertheless follows an individual path that is in part determined by its own reactions as it develops. His theory helps us understand, too, why so much that the early proponents of "artificial intelligence" predicted has simply not come to pass. These ingenious, sometimes brilliant specialists in computer science were working with a picture of the brain that reflected, not true disorderly reality, but an abstract, even a mechanistic neurology that biology now completely rejects. Those working with artificial intelligence have begun to take this into account, too, though sometimes partially and sometimes, I suspect, also reluctantly, for those who are drawn to order can find it hard to accept the inevitability of disorder.

The parallels with contemporary procedures in the arts seem irresistible. We do not need to go as far as John Cage and pretty much abandon all order: life can be irregular without being fully aleatory. But would Igor Stravinsky or Arnold Schoenberg have rejected Gleick's claim that "life sucks order from a sea of disorder" (299)? Johann Sebastian Bach might well have rejected it out of hand, as Ludwig van Beethoven probably would have and, though with less certainty and conviction, so too Johannes Brahms. But would Richard Wagner have disagreed with Gleick? I don't want to stop to debate the question. The point is, surely, that the closer we come to our own time, the less resistance to theories like those described by Gleick are we likely to find. What is remarkable in the following passage, from a letter written by Joseph Conrad almost a hundred years ago, is the exceedingly casual, indeed flippant way in which the worldview of modern science has been absorbed:

> All day with the ship-owners and in the evening dinner, phonograph, X rays, talk about *the* secret of the Universe and the nonexistence of, so called, matter. The secret of the universe is in the existence of horizontal waves whose varied vibrations are at the bottom of all states of consciousness. If the waves were vertical the universe would be different. This is a truism. But, don't you see, there is nothing in the world to prevent the simultaneous existence of vertical waves, of waves at any angles; in fact there are mathematical reasons for believing that such waves do exist. Therefore it follows that two universes may exist in the same place and in the same time—and not only two universes but an infinity of different universes. . . . And, note, *all* [the universes] composed of the same matter, matter, *all matter* being only that thing of inconceivable tenuity through which the various vibrations of waves (electricity, heat, sound, light etc.) are propagated, thus giving birth to our sensations—then emotions—then thought. (143; emphasis in original)

Conrad's mockingly playful version of modern science ends with his hope to conclude a particular business arrangement shortly. "If I don't," he reports, "I shall vanish into space (there's no space) and the vibrations that make me up, shall go into the making of some other fool" (144). More than seventy years later, in a letter to a neurophysiologist, the novelist John Dos Passos records a very similar fascination with the difference between how science sees the world and the visible world that all men see: "I would say that in later life Bertrand Russell became an intolerant materialist. I dont know much about modern astrophysics but my impression is that Russells cosmogony has been completely demolished. What about the hypothetical universes made necessary by modern mathematics" (641)? Again, the striking fact is how deeply the views of science have penetrated, and interpenetrated, the lives of literary people.

Even those who scoffed and tried as hard as they could not to comprehend were forced to admit the power and importance of the scientific view. Science might not be trusted, but it could not be ignored. Writing from the Paris Exposition of 1900, Henry Adams assured John Hay (himself at one time personal secretary to President Abraham Lincoln):

> I can already see that the scientific theories and laws of our generation will, to the next, appear as antiquated as the Ptolemaic system. . . . The charm of the [exposition], to me, is that no one pretends to understand even in a remote degree, what these weird things are that they call electricity, Roentgen rays [i.e., X rays], and what not. The exhibitors are dead dumped into infinity on a fork. (*Letters, 1892–1918*, 301)

Ten years earlier still, Adams filled his letters with mocking references to Charles Darwin's theory of coral reefs—but went on trying as hard as he could to refute them, working diligently to gather facts that would prove Darwin wrong.

> Darwin says that the coral islands have miraculous powers of sinking, while all the coral islands I have seen are perfectly stupid evidences of rising. Till now I have never seen or heard of a clear case of rise more than perhaps two or three hundred feet. Here [Fiji] they claim a thousand feet or more of it. If we can settle this, I give you all the advantages. The next time you meet a geologist you can hit him on the head with my specimens. . . . (*Letters, 1858–1891*, 499)

So too H. L. Mencken, writing to the novelist Upton Sinclair in 1930, poked fun at Einstein and others who, in his view, held credulous opinions on the subject of parapsychological phenomena. "It is a well known fact," he wrote bitingly, "that physicists are greatly given to the supernatural. Why this should be I don't know, but the fact is plain. . . . I have the suspicion that the cause may be that physics itself, as currently practised, is largely moonshine" (*Letters*, 322). And even those who neither believed nor scoffed, but followed their own paths and looked around with some wonder at what science was saying, tried at least to harmonize the views of science with their own approach. William Butler Yeats, for one, found Alfred North Whitehead's universe very like his own. Writing to Ezra Pound's mother-in-law, in 1926, he says:

> I have found a very difficult but profound person[,] Whitehead, who seems to have reached my own conclusions about ultimate things. He has written down the game of chess and I, like some Italian Prince, have made the pages and the court ladies have it out on the lawn. Not that he would recognise his abstract triumph in my gay rabble. . . . [Whitehead] thinks that nothing exists but "organisms," or minds . . . and that there is no such thing as an object "localized in space," except the minds, and that which we call physical objects of all kinds are "aspects" or "vistas" of other "organisms." . . . He also uses the "Quantum Theory" when speaking of minute organisms—molecules. . . . (712–14)

Plainly, Yeats understands relatively little; he sees only what he chooses to see. But he clearly understands the power of scientific validation, if he can possibly manage to find it.

Scientific truth as we have come to see it (again, in Gleick's words) is that, just as artists do, "Nature forms patterns. Some," as he observes, "are orderly in space but disorderly in time, others orderly in time but disorderly in space" (308). I suspect that any critic of contemporary literature and the other arts would at once acknowledge this as an obvious truism. And could a contemporary biologist disagree with Gleick, when he quotes with complete approval the physicist Joseph Ford: "Evolution is chaos with feedback" (314)? I do not think Gerald Edelman would disagree: Ford's statement seems to me virtually a paraphrase of Edelman's *Neural Darwinism.*

Our discussion of the interrelationships between science and literature therefore takes on a somewhat different cast. And as I have said, scientists as well as literary folk have had to come to terms with the nonlinear, whether they wanted to or not. More than a quarter of a century ago the physicist Henry Margenau, writing jointly with the philosopher J. E. Smith, summed up the three revolutions of twentieth-century science:

> One is the progressive revelation that matter . . . is much less solid, uniform, and simple than was originally supposed. . . . Next . . . is a group of facts indicating a failure of the continuity of motion in the atomic world. . . . And thirdly, we must recall certain developments that draw into question a principle ordinarily called causality, a principle whose rejection is sometimes said to entail freedom. (382)

Richard Ford, once again, sums up these three revolutions in singularly pithy terms: "Relativity eliminated the Newtonian illusion of absolute space and time; quantum theory eliminated the Newtonian dream of a controllable measurement process; and [now] chaos eliminates the Laplacian fantasy of deterministic predictability" (Gleick, 6). Ford's words toll exactly like the language employed by many contemporary writers—and musicians and painters and sculptors. Illusions, dreams, and fantasies are frequently just what all our contemporary arts simultaneously mourn and celebrate. "The twentieth century," writes Walter Sorell, "is characterized by . . . radical changes in the approach to and concepts of the arts. . . . Experiments follow one another with ever-growing acceleration. There can be no doubt that we are about to destroy the heritage which Renaissance man dreamed of and created . . ." (42). But whatever it is we destroy or do not destroy, we must recognize that we are proceeding as we must, voluntarily and inevitably. "The more an artist is 'true to himself,' " declares yet another Nobel Prize winner, the Greek poet George Seferis,

> the more completely will he instill his own time into his work. The bond between the artist and his time is not an intellectual one. . . . It is rather the umbilical cord that connects mother and child, a purely biological attachment. . . . Out of this human condition, in its madnesses and in its silences, what elements will he conserve? What must he conserve and what must he turn his back upon out of all this amorphous human material, which is terrifyingly alive . . . ? (195–96)

How then do scientists think, in our intellectually and emotionally disordered time, when they practice science? "If we understand a hypothesis as the perception of some pattern in phenomena, the establishment of some expectation as to what will happen next," argue Martin and Inge Goldstein in *How We Know*, "we realize that 'forming hypotheses' is something we do all the time and have been doing since birth." And the Goldsteins (both of them practicing research scientists) add: "Because scientific discovery has this character, one should not be surprised to learn that it is not a routine, mechanical process but rather one in which the subconscious mind plays a part (as it does in artistic creativity, also) and that chance and circumstance contribute" (242–43). As James D. Watson puts it, in his now-famous account of the discovery of DNA, *The Double Helix*, "As I hope this book will show, science seldom proceeds in the straightforward logical manner imagined by outsiders. Instead, its steps forwards (and sometimes backward) are often very human events in which personalities and cultural traditions play major roles. . . . Styles of scientific research vary almost as much as human personalities" (ix). Or as Thomas S. Kuhn declares, "An apparently arbitrary element, compounded of personal and historical accident, is always a formative ingredient of the beliefs espoused by a given scientific community at a given time" (4). Lewis S. Feuer goes still further: "Emotions determine the perspective, the framework, for the explanation of the perceived world. . . . The source of scientific creativity has always been a spirit of play . . ." (1, 12). Or as Albert Einstein bluntly phrased it:

> [Ernst] Mach's weakness, as I see it, lies in the fact that he believed more or less strongly, that science consists merely

of putting experimental results in order, that is, he did not recognize the free constructive elements in the creation of a concept. He thought that somehow theories arise by means of *discovery* and not by means of *invention*. (Miller, *Imagery*, 4)

Only scientists can follow all the steps in scientific procedure; frequently the very notation of science, and especially its mathematics, is a formidable barrier for the nonscientist. Without in fact being scientists, and participating in the actual processes of scientific investigation, the best we can do is to eavesdrop on scientists at work. But though a great deal of science is incredibly intricate and specialized, there is also much that is almost elementary, once the basic principles are grasped. It is hardly accidental that one of the greatest scientists of our time, and surely the most famous, Albert Einstein, frequently worked completely in his head, not resorting to any complex apparatus, and reducing his *Gedanken*, or "Thought Experiments," to principles that are fairly readily understandable. Einstein's relativity theory, for example, emerged from a 1905 *Gedanken*-style experiment that, though it had taken ten years to work through, was entirely mental and was, furthermore, in its essence neither complex nor hard to grasp.

Picture an experimenter who is moving forward, pursuing a specific point located on a wave of light. Catching up to it, he measures different velocities of light. As physics understood matters in 1905, the experimenter could himself achieve light's velocity, so the light would seem to him like a standing wave. But Einstein intuited that the laws of optics could not be dependent on how fast the moving experimenter was moving. This visualization presented the opposing possibilities in very plain form, and Einstein resolved the situation equally plainly. Time, he reasoned, was absolute, but our measurements of it were not and could not be: we were necessarily limited to partial and forever inaccurate measurements. The power and importance of this apparently simple perception is enormous: from 1905 to today, it has been reverberating through science, philosophy, and virtually all aspects of human thought, changing not simply the way we think but also the way we design and build and work in the physical universe that surrounds us.

Arthur I. Miller, in his closely researched and densely written study, *Imagery in Scientific Thought*, nicely links music, mathematics, and the thought processes of Albert Einstein, as I have just briefly summarized them:

> Mental imagery in auditory, sensual, and visual modes has played a central role in creative thought. Wolfgang Amadeus Mozart's auditory imagery permitted him to hear a new symphony "tout ensemble" [all at once]. The great French mathematician and philosopher Henri Poincaré's "sensual imagery" led him to sense a mathematical proof in its entirety "at a glance." Albert Einstein's creative thinking occurred in visual imagery, and words were "sought after laboriously only in a secondary stage." (221)

Ifor Evans, in *Literature and Science*, similarly describes the process by which, "at its highest, imagery, by drawing together widely separated objects and experiences . . . , asserts the unity of human life" (112–13). Yet Evans is not here talking of science, but of poetry. And ask yourself of whom he speaks when, at the very end of his book, he urges the practitioner to "remember that whatever power and dignity may surround other disciplines his . . . is the nearest approach to an interpretation that man has of the nature of his own experience given in terms of that experience" (113). I think very few scientists would reject that as a description of science's mission; I suspect most, but by no means all, writers would subscribe to it as a description of theirs. Evans was in fact talking about writers, not scientists, and our inability to immediately tell in which direction he was facing seems to me enormously revealing. Wylie Sypher points out, in *Literature and Technology*, that "one uses the terms technology, science, and art only under duress, for in fact there are only technicians, scientists, and artists . . ." (xx). Sypher goes on, toward the end of his book, to observe approvingly that recently

> there has been a *rapprochement* between the arts and science in that both have returned to thinking with the body. . . . The following generations [i.e., those after Newton] forgot what Newton himself and other great

scientific minds knew, that their discoveries were, to them, a kind of play, the free exercise of a mind driven by curiosity and eagerness that resembles the Dionysiac spirit. . . . The revolution in the recent arts and in recent science is basically due to the fact that the notion of art and science as imitation has been displaced by the notion of art and science as participation. (180, 199, 201)

As Herbert Butterfield observes, in his *Origins of Modern Science*:

> in both celestial and terrestrial physics . . . change is brought about, not by new observations or additional evidence in the first instance, but by transpositions that were taking place inside the minds of the scientists themselves. In this connection it is not irrelevant to note that, of all forms of mental activity, the most difficult to induce even in the minds of the young, who may be presumed not to have lost their flexibility, is the art of handling the same bundle of data as before, but placing them in a new system of relations with one another by giving them a different framework. (13)

Again, it is plain that these exact things can be said, have been said, and are being said today about fields other than "celestial and terrestrial physics." "I wonder," ruminates the poet Allen Ginsberg, "to what extent does the science that we have . . . reflect scientific method? To what extent is it an absolute, inevitable product of its own presuppositions, independent research and pure fact?" His answer, which we have seen is not far wrong, is that "science itself is pure magic, really, and it's just pure wish-fulfillment, whichever direction it goes" (*Allen Verbatim*, 213, 222).

But Ginsberg's error is that he finds the "pure magic" of poetry wonderfully acceptable while rejecting the "pure magic" of science. He is certainly not alone. In a letter written in 1900, George Bernard Shaw pokes fun at the "doctrine of Omniscience and Infallibility as regards Science," which doctrine he affirms is "precisely the same kind as the old doctrine as to Religion." Referring to the "precise calculations" of science, Shaw insists that this is "pure miracle-gaping megalomania. . . . The agreement among the physicists as to the measurements is as imaginary as the agreement about nitrogen, oxygen and carbon dioxide accounting for the atmosphere." Science, he urges, must be gotten "on to a purely secular plane" (176–78). Not many scientists would disagree with Shaw's verdict; many would also agree with his comment to H. G. Wells, the next year, "that the difference, so far, between the Pentateuch and the scriptures of the scientific materialism of the sixties, is the difference between shrewd nonsense and DAMNED nonsense" (246). But the degree of skepticism shown by Ginsberg is not the majority view held by poets and novelists. For one thing, it is impossible not to see that science has not only dominated and even shaped man's horizon but has entered into everyday literary speech as well as into hordes of literary volumes. "At present," the playwright Sean O'Casey wrote to a friend in 1927, "I'm busily engaged trying to solve an Einstein problem of how to buy a 4000 pound house for 25 shillings" (221). This is Einstein very fuzzily comprehended, but the significance of the usage remains. Thomas Mann came a good deal closer to a proper Einsteinian appreciation, confessing in a 1932 letter that "the musings on time in *The Magic Mountain*" had unfortunately been grasped only "ideally," without the proper sense of physical reality that would have been at his disposal if when he wrote that great novel he had, as he had not, read Einstein (192).

But for a more integrated sense of what science means to those who live the literary rather than the scientific life, we need to turn to writers like D. H. Lawrence. Lawrence is not a scholar of anything, but he is an intensely practical writer, concerned with trying to change society and the individuals who compose it. His creed was an aggressive, dedicated vitalism: his books speak, still, with the passionate conviction of an absolutely determined lover of this world and all things and people in it. And though he was often vague on details, and just as often dead wrong in judgments of both people and ideas (Lawrence was sometimes one of the least patient men who ever lived), he also understood many basic things in great depth. As he wrote to Bertrand Russell, "For heaven's sake don't think . . . be a baby, and not a savant any more. Don't *do* anything any more—but for heaven's sake begin to *be*—start at the very beginning and be a perfect baby: in the name of courage" (*Psychoanalysis and the Unconscious*, xv). In a long essay, "Education of the People," Lawrence amplifies this notion of innocent understanding in ways that demonstrate how much a part of himself scientific notions and also scientific knowledge had become:

> The body is not an instrument, but a living organism. . . . We must look to the great affective centres, emotional and volitional. . . . [And] the two chief emotional centres in the baby are the solar plexus of the abdomen and the cardiac plexus of the breast. The corresponding ganglia of the volitional system are the lumbar ganglion and the thoracic ganglion. . . . The brain at first acts only as a switchboard which keeps these active centres in circuit of communication. . . . Mental activity, final cognition, ideation, is only set up secondarily from the perfect interaction and intercommunication of the primary affective centres. . . . (*Phoenix*, 618–20)

Lawrence did not like Freud's psychology. Not understanding it particularly well, he thought Freud's work excessively rationalist—that is, employing the stiff, formal logic that was anathema to Lawrence's very being. But underneath both the vast scene of Freudian psychology, and the powerfully ranging insights of Lawrence's fiction and other writing, there remains an approach that must I think be termed fundamentally scientific. Lawrence's "Education of the People" is in no way unique in the corpus of his writing. He was always driving as hard as he knew how toward the truth as he was able to understand it—toward, if you will, a melding of experience and thought, of experiment and theory. Writing just after the French Revolution, Bernard Lacépède, in closing the course on zoology that he gave at the Muséum d'histoire naturelle in Paris, exclaimed that human disaster could only be prevented "if we unite the liberal arts, which embody the sacred fire of sensibility, with the sciences and the useful arts, without which the celestial light of reason will disappear" (quoted in Stephen Jay Gould, "The Passion of Antoine Lavoisier," *Natural History*, June 1989, 25).

Was Lawrence any more impulsive, indeed, than Enrico Fermi,

who discovered the effect of slow neutrons on induced radioactivity by an utterly spontaneous change in experimental procedure? Fermi himself has recorded how this came about:

> We were working very hard on the neutron-induced radioactivity and the results we were obtaining made no sense. One day, as I came to the laboratory, it occurred to me that I should examine the effect of placing a piece of lead before the incident neutrons. Instead of my usual custom, I took great pains to have the piece of lead precisely machined. I was clearly dissatisfied with something; I tried every excuse to postpone putting the piece of lead in its place. When finally, with some reluctance, I was going to put it in place, I said to myself: "No, I do not want this piece of lead here; what I want is a piece of paraffin." It was just like that, *with no advance warning, no conscious prior reasoning*. I immediately took some odd piece of paraffin and placed it where the piece of lead was to have been. (Chandrasekhar, 21; emphasis added)

This last-minute, totally unplanned substitution of paraffin for lead turned out to be what made the experiment successful.

So too the nineteeth-century German chemist Friedrich Kekulé, who made large contributions to the theoretical structures of organic chemistry, had been wrestling for some time with the structural patterns of carbon atoms when they joined with other elements. Again, he has himself recorded how he came to understand that carbon atoms could provide the essential backbone of complex organic compounds by joining to themselves in long chains or rings:

> One fine summer evening, I was returning by the last omnibus, "outside" as usual, through the deserted streets of the metropolis, which are at other times so full of life. I fell into a reverie, and lo! the atoms were gamboling before my eyes. Whenever, hitherto, these diminutive beings had appeared to me, they had always been in motion; but up to that time, I had never been able to discern the nature of their motion. Now, however, I saw how, frequently, two

smaller atoms united to form a pair; how a larger one embraced two smaller ones; how still larger ones kept hold of three or even four of the smaller; whilst the whole kept whirling in a giddy dance. I saw how the larger ones formed a chain. . . . I spent part of the night putting on paper at least sketches of these dream forms. (Goldstein and Goldstein, 194)

Nor was this a onetime method used by Kekulé to discover scientific truths. He records that another time

I turned my chair before the fire and dozed. Again the atoms were gamboling before my eyes. This time the smaller groups kept modestly in the background. My mental eye, rendered more acute by repeated visions of the kind, could not distinguish larger structures, of manifold conformation; long rows, sometimes more closely fitted together; all twining and twisting in snakelike motion. But look! What was that? One of the snakes had seized hold of its own tail, and the form whirled mockingly before my eyes. As if by a flash of lightning I awoke. . . . (ibid.)

Isaac Asimov, a professional biochemist as well as a writer of science fiction, has speculated that it may have been because of Kekulé's early training as an architectural student that he was able to have these kinds of structural insights. But Kekulé was the furthest thing from irrational or unbalanced. Asimov notes that although there has been a good deal of subsequent refinement of Kekulé's work, its essence remains valid and, indeed, "has guided chemists through the maze of synthesis for a century and despite all modifications still serves to depict the organic molecule and to help predict its reactions" (447–48).

How different, indeed, is Kekulé's method from that attributed to the plant geneticist Barbara McClintock?

Over and over again, she tells us one must have the time to look, the patience to "hear what the material has to say to you," the openness to "let it come to you. . . . An organism

> isn't just a piece of plastic, it's something that is constantly being affected by the environment. . . ."

"Good science," continues McClintock's biographer, Evelyn Fox Keller (herself a mathematician and biologist),

> cannot proceed without a deep emotional investment on the part of the scientist. . . . Over the years, a special kind of sympathetic understanding grew in McClintock, heightening her powers of discernment, until finally, the objects of her study have become subjects in their own right; they claim from her a kind of attention that most of us experience only in relation to other persons. (198, 200)

As Keller also says, "The nature of insight in science . . . is notoriously elusive. And almost all great scientists—those who learn to cultivate insight—learn also to respect its mysterious workings. . . . In defying rational explanation, the process of creative insight inspires awe in those who experience it. They come to know, trust, and value it" (103). Another geneticist, C. H. Waddington, emphatically agrees: "It is time," he insists, "that scientists become willing to state explicitly that the scientific attitude is as full of passion, as much a function of the whole man and not merely of an intellectual part of him, as any other approach to human action" (33).

Yet how different from such approaches is the description given by the novelist Joyce Cary, in a fine and too-little-known book, *Art and Reality*? "All great artists," he says, "are preoccupied, as if by nature, with reality. They assume, from the beginning, that it is their task to reveal a truth about some permanent and fundamental real." In his essay "The Function of the Novelist," Cary rephrased this formulation in a manner that I think most scientists would heartily endorse: "The function of the novel . . . is to make the world contemplate and understand itself, not only as rational being but as experience of value, as a complete thing" (*Essays*, 153). Trained as a painter before he became a writer, Cary makes it clear that what he is saying is in his judgment "true of all the arts":

> The work of art as completely realised is the result of a long and complex process of exploration, as well as construction. This is true even of a painter. The notion that a painter suddenly imagines a composition . . . and straightway puts it down, is untrue. He begins with a general idea, no doubt. . . . But he has not yet got color and form on canvas, he has not translated . . . actual fields and trees into symbols and, however experienced he is, he does not know exactly how to get the effects he wants, or even if it is possible within the limits of his material. He proceeds by trial and error. . . . Manet would scrape off his paint day after day until, after fifty trials, he could satisfy himself that no further improvement was possible. That is, he was not merely expressing an intuition, he was continually discovering new possibilities in his own work, now become objective to him, and realising them. (103)

The "new possibilities" Joyce Cary refers to are supremely the goal of the science-fiction writer, who is virtually by definition testing such possibilities all the time—new worlds, new technologies, new races and beings. Even when he spins back into the past, via one or another time-travel device, the science-fiction writer is concerned with remaking that past and creating new possibilities for it. This is of course not the place for either a full or even a strictly historical treatment of science fiction. Nor do I wish to hurriedly and superficially condescend to a genre for which I have immense respect and that, most soberly, I regard as of very great importance for the future development of fiction. But as the literary form most responsive to scientific developments and ways of thought, science fiction simply requires our attention: it seems to me the logical closing point for this discussion.

We are in fact dealing with an older and more established, and better established, genre than is sometimes realized. Mary Shelley's *Frankenstein*, written almost two centuries ago, is hardly the first science-fiction novel, any more than Isaac Newton, dead just about a century before that novel's publication, was the first scientist. And there is fine and interesting work in related fields, notably the fantasy novel, which dates back centuries further. (Perhaps the most significant recent exemplar of the fantasy novel, distinguished from science fiction precisely because it does *not* involve new possibilities so much as a blurring of the boundaries surrounding accepted reality, is J. R. R. Tolkien's *Lord of the Rings*.) Accordingly, to help keep these final remarks in reasonable focus, I want to briefly discuss just three books: Frank Herbert's *Dune* (1965), Walter M. Miller, Jr.'s, magnificent *A Canticle for Leibowitz* (1959), and a tautly drawn collaborative novel, Larry Niven and Jerry Pournelle's *Mote in God's Eye* (1974).

Let me simply note, preliminarily, that I have been reading science fiction since the late 1930s, when eagerly awaited monthly issues of what seemed to me the best magazine in the world, *Astounding Science Fiction*, sold for the very steep price of twenty-five cents (a price the publishers could safely charge not only because they had the best science fiction going, but also because they had replaced the pulp paper and sloppy typefaces featured in lesser journals with sharp-edged typefaces and with paper that did not smudge when you looked at it). I should perhaps also note that my own science-fiction stories began to appear in print in 1960, the first one debuting in *Fantasy and Science Fiction*. I speak, that is, on the basis of long and intensive reading, and also from hands-on experience.

It must be said at once that neither the structure nor the writing of *Dune* is much different, or in any significant way superior, to that of much other science fiction. Herbert writes clean, efficient prose; he does not aspire to literary excellence, and when he does soar, modestly, he is apt to rely on rather stock phrases and descriptions. But as I have argued elsewhere, notably in discussing *The Lord of the Rings*, which is also a massively marvelous book of strictly limited technical literary achievement (stock prose, bad poetry, standard characters, standard plot lines), what *does* set *Dune* (like *The Lord of the Rings*) apart is its conception, the vast, broadly based and symbolically charged values it grandly and energetically embodies. *Dune* is in fact an extended metaphor for the ecological, and thus the moral and political, problems of our world. Herbert makes a straightforward futuristic projection, grafting onto his imagined new world those virtues that he wishes to be enhanced and ultimately to prevail in our own existence. That, in a word, is the methodology of most science fiction, as also it is the governing mind-set of many practicing scientists. Why else, indeed, would Robert Oppenheimer, as he watched man's first controlled atomic explosion, recall lines from the *Bhagavad Gita*: "I am become Death, the destroyer of worlds"? Courage is a splendid thing, in *Dune*, but as it is in our own world, it is also a fragile thing, that can be bought off, that can be diverted, that can be completely subverted. There is continuous, passionate, intelligent exploration of the newness of the new and yet timeless situation around which the book is built. That too is what science is all about, and it is precisely why *Dune* fully deserves the adjectival modifier in the genre's name: this is indeed *science* fiction.

A Canticle for Leibowitz is perhaps the finest, as well as the most literary, science-fiction novel published in this country. It is also the only novel Walter M. Miller, Jr., has ever written. Born in 1923, he began by writing stories, many of them first-rate, none of them so complex and far-ranging as this book; once he had finished *A Canticle for Leibowitz* he withdrew from both writing and the public world, reappearing only quite recently, but not yet (and perhaps never again) as a writer.

Miller's approach too is futuristic, based this time on an evaluation of what science as practiced by human beings seems likely to lead to. He postulates the almost total destruction of mankind, and an accompanying loss of scientific as well as other knowledge, in a nuclear holocaust. Centuries later, stored but not understood by the still-thriving Catholic church, documents revealing the secrets of scientific knowledge are found; centuries later still, these Memorabilia, as the church terms them, are sought out by "minds ready to be kindled" (143). Slowly, slowly, science-dominated civilization more or less as we have known it is reborn. Then, very quickly, just as it did the first time, that science-dominated civilization destroys itself in atomic warfare. Carefully set against science's intensely secular, amoral values, however, is the eternal understanding of religion. "Are we doomed to it, Lord," a priest asks, "chained to the pendulum of our own mad clockwork, helpless to halt its swing" (255)? The answer, clearly, is both yes and no—for though the world is well on its way to a second destruction (or a third, if we take Noah's Flood as seriously as do the monks of the Order of the Blessed Leibowitz), mankind also starts down two pathways that may in fact check the pendulum's swinging. First, the assorted monstrosities spawned by radiation may, this time, be spawning a new and, hopefully, a better race of men. Second, with the knowledge of the first atomic destruction in mind, the church has this time prepared a spaceship, to be dispatched to an earth colony on Alpha Centaurus, there to found both a new church and, in essence, a new world. The final benediction and instructions to the crew of this spaceship goes, in part, like this:

> You will be years in space. The ship will be your monastery. After the patriarchal see is established at the Centaurus Colony, you will found there a mother house of the Visitationist Friars of the Order of Saint Leibowitz of Tycho. But the ship will remain in your hands, and the Memorabilia. If civilization, or a vestige of it, can maintain itself on Centaurus, you will send missions to the other colony worlds, and perhaps eventually to the colonies of their colonies. Wherever Man goes, you and your successors will go. And with you, the records and remembrances of four thousand years and more. . . . Be for Man the memory of Earth and Origin. Remember this Earth. Never forget her, but—*never come back.* . . . If you ever [do] come back, you might meet the Archangel at the east end of Earth, guarding her passes with a sword of flame. (277)

Obviously, Miller's prose is cadenced and honed beyond the imagining of Frank Herbert. And the novel is full of obvious comprehension both of the nature of science, often in elaborate detail, and of the nature of man. The characters are subtly, profoundly drawn; the intricate subplotting is handled without clichés or easy predictability.

I include Niven and Pournelle's *Mote in God's Eye* because it too, like *Dune,* is built around a singularly potent, large-scale conception. Its characters are all too obviously machines for energizing that conception, rather than individuals in their own right. The writing, though neither sloppy nor uncontrolled, lacks the full-fledged bite of Miller's prose or even the crispness of Herbert's sometimes stylized patternings. These are all substantive matters; they affect the book's ultimate value, and I do not mean to discount them. But with all its flaws, *The Mote in God's Eye* is shaped by serious, thoughtful, moral concern for the ethical implications of a breakthrough long heralded and dreamed, namely, man's first encounter with an intelligent species totally different from our own. The pitfalls and opportunities of such a confrontation, as well as mankind's advantages and disadvantages in conducting it, are sensitively explored. The book presents these still-hypothetical problems vividly, making them living, three-dimensional, palpable, and even pressing issues in a way that more formal discussions have failed to do.

That, in a word, is the power of art, as it is also the reason for this book—bearing, let me remind you, the overall title *Artists All*. At the end of the essay from which I have borrowed Bernard Lacépède's remarks, and immediately after quoting them, Stephen Jay Gould concludes with these ringing words: "The Republic needs scientists." It is my job to add to Gould's invocation that the Republic, and Science, also need Art.

4

LITERATURE
AND
MUSIC

The ancient symbiosis of music and literature is both as old and as powerful as that between mother and child. There are, of course, no prehistorical records of either of these primitive bonds, but all the evidence we have indicates that, just as speech and literature were evolving in the early years of *Homo sapiens* (and probably in such predecessor species as Neanderthal man), music was evolving along with them, interdependently, almost interchangeably. Our language is full of references to poetry as music, but musical language need not be in poetic form. Music-and-word linkages are so completely, inherently fundamental, so utterly basic that composers cannot usually tell you why they choose one text and refuse another. "My . . . reaction to poetry is instant: this is for me, this is not for me," writes the composer Robert Starer. "Sometimes I even hear music the first time I read a poem" (118). The linkages are so fundamental that, as the composer Virgil

Thomson says, music and words "are mated, not just living together" (13). Or as Robert Starer explains the relationship, and the genesis of music out of words, "vocal music is derived from language" (63).

But verbalization *about* music is necessarily a different matter. A composer's most significant reaction to a verbal text occurs in his own language—that is, in music, which like verbal languages can be heard but unlike verbal languages has meaning only in terms of itself. For a composer to talk about music in someone else's language, the verbalizations that we are accustomed to calling language, can be daunting. The composer George Crumb insists:

> I think music is a language in its own right. I think healthy periods in music avoided this verbalization; it was enough for them to write the music and play it. Criticism, you know, in the nineteenth century didn't become an analytical intellectual approach to music; it was rather a poetic reaction to music.
>
> I think it's the only sensible way to react to music. (*Artists as Professors*, 47)

This is a common stance among music professionals. I vividly recall discussing piano literature with a young pianist, more than forty years ago. Whenever I made normative judgments, and pressed him to agree or disagree, he would smile mildly and say, "Well, it's all music, you know. It isn't a question of better or worse. It's just different, that's all."

Musicians are of course correct: music *is* a language in its own right. Virgil Thomson says of musical drama that, without exception,

> the story line is dependent on music for its pacing. A verbal text needs to be heard without effort, but the continuity that controls our attention is the musical one. . . . The words are always there, of course; . . . emotionally and factually they may seem to be telling their own story, but in reality they are doing very little more than to explain the music. By the very nature of musical reception, its unbeliev-

able speed and intensity as compared to [verbal] language, a piece of vocal music is primarily music. (26, 48)

Thomson also says, brilliantly:

> If songs really need words (as indeed they mostly do, since the human voice without them is just another wind instrument) then there has to be in the marriage of words and music a basic compatibility in which the text's exact shape and purpose dominate the union, or seem to. I say seem to, because actually a large part of music's contribution lies in the emotional timings, the urgencies about continuity, the whole pacing and moving forwardness of the composition *that only music can provide*. (1–2; emphasis added)

All the same, when we talk about music we are obliged to use the language of words. And the language of music not only makes use of but very deliberately, and completely volitionally, enters into an extremely close relationship with the language of words whenever it chooses to provide musical settings for literary texts. This intimate relationship with verbal language also occurs, though somewhat less specifically, when music uses literary ideas and associations as its own starting point (and often for its descriptive titles or sectional indications, as well). Since most people are not musicians, talk about music is almost always nontechnical, but again, whether technical or not, it is inevitably talk, that is, the language of words, verbal rather than musical. This can sometimes put musicians on the defensive. Roger Sessions argues passionately that music is not "a vague and imprecise means of communication . . . ," though

> I have frequently heard such views expressed, especially by people working primarily in other media, and most often by literary people. . . . [But] it seems to me quite clear that music, far from being in any sense vague or imprecise, is *within its own sphere* the most precise possible language. . . . It achieves a meaning which can be conveyed no other way. (23–24; emphasis added)

Deryck Cooke entitles his exposition of musical fundamentals *The Language of Music*, and immediately attacks the question of music's true expressive powers. Is music, he asks, "a genuine emotional language, whose terms actually possess the inherent power to awaken certain definite emotions in the listener, or is it [only] a collection of *formulae* attached by habit over a long period to certain verbally explicit emotions in masses, operas, and songs, which produce in the listener a series of conditioned reflexes?" Cooke too is defensive, though his answer to the question is almost extravagantly affirmative. Indeed, the basic purpose of his book is to combat any narrow assessment of music's powers. "Music is a language of the emotions," he insists, and quite as emotional as literature, since "both make use of a language of sounds for the purpose of expression. . . . Music is no more incapable of being emotionally intelligible because it is bound by the laws of musical construction, than poetry is because it is bound by the laws of verbal grammatical construction." Cooke deliberately pitches his argument in the widest possible terms:

> When we try to assess the achievement of a great literary artist, one of the chief ways in which we approach his work is to examine it as a report on human experience. We feel that, in his art, he has said something significant in relation to life as it is lived; and that what he has said . . . is as important as the purely formal aspect of his writing. . . . The same is unfortunately not felt to be true of the artist who makes his contribution to human culture, not in the language of speech, but in that of music. Music is widely regarded nowadays, not as a language at all, but as a "pure," inexpressive art . . . and even those who do feel it to be some kind of language regard it as an imprecise one, incapable of conveying anything so tangible as an experience of life or an attitude towards it. (ix, 24, 25, 31)

Perhaps because, unlike Roger Sessions, he had immediate success not only as a composer but also as a pianist and conductor, Leonard Bernstein looked at music's powers of expression through the large rather than the small end of the telescope. Bernstein was also verbally gifted: he spoke many languages, and spoke them

well, and he wrote easily and clearly. Accordingly, rather than
being defensive about music as a language in its own right, he is
distinctly arrogant:

> For some reason literary minds sccm magnctized by musi-
> cal terminology—probably because they are awe-struck by
> the abstractness of it all. Nothing can be more different
> from the representational literary mind, with its literal
> conceptuality, than the non-objective musical mind, with
> its concentration on shapes, lines, and sonorous intensities.
> And this fascinates the writer—makes him even a little
> envious, I have found—so that he longs for some partici-
> pation in that strange, foreign medium. . . . [But] *the only
> way one can really say anything about music is to write
> music.* (15, 13; emphasis added)

Yet the entire argument about what music is capable of *saying*
is plainly somewhat circular. Much if not everything depends on
how the crucial terms are defined and also on what one wants to
prove. Having set out my own view a quarter of a century ago, in
an essay entitled "Music, Poetry, and Translation," let me simply
quote myself for a moment:

> Both music and poetry are, in a sense, languages within
> languages. Organized sound—perhaps the broadest defini-
> tion of music—is scarcely ever a communications system
> in the way that words are: music speaks, to be sure, but if
> its message is to be translated into verbal terms only the
> most elementary expressions are recognizable. But in the
> manipulation of its proper component parts—pitch,
> rhythm, instrumental color, dynamics, and the like—music
> is closely analogous to speech. To capable musicians, in-
> deed, the expressions of musical communication are apt to
> be as meaningful as strictly verbal statements. . . . For
> poets and composers both, the variations and combina-
> tions are endless; each in his own particularized language
> can "say" as much as he personally is capable of. (*The
> Forked Tongue*, 154)

A year or two after writing that essay, which categorizes both poetry and music as subdivisions of larger orders—poetry a subdivision of verbal language, music a subdivision of the world of sounds—I happened to be at a party where the avant-garde composer John Cage was approached by someone totally unaware of his work, who asked what he did. "I'm interested in noise," said Cage with a cheerful smile.

I propose to discuss music's relationships with literature as they operate in two opposite directions: first, and primarily, the influence of literature on music, and second, and more briefly, the influence of music on literature. Let me begin with the larger of these two broad topics, literature's influence on music, which in its turn can be divided into two very different subcategories: one, providing texts for musical setting, whether libretti specifically intended for a composer to set to music or a text that a composer comes across and appropriates for his own purposes; and two, providing the less-specific programmatic subject matter, or general mood, or starting point, that triggers musical composition. I will begin with literature's influence on music, but the subject is so very large that I cannot hope to finish even a fairly compact commentary in one chapter, so that I will not get to music's influence on literature until well along in chapter 5.

Since virtually all song texts, and most libretti, are in verse, I need to say a few preliminary things about poetic versus musical prosody. As far as poetic prosody is concerned, I will limit myself to the English language. I am well aware that the prosody of a stress-phonemic language like English—that is, a language where a change in stress can produce a change in meaning—is different from the prosody of a syllabic language like French, and is even less like either the prosody of a tonal language like Chinese or a quantitative one like classical Latin. And word rhythm in a language plainly affects musical composition based on texts from that language. Robert Starer says, succinctly, "when I follow Hebrew word rhythm I write different music than when I follow English word rhythm" (43). Or as Virgil Thomson puts it, "The only fatal procedure is to forget that English is one of the most varied and expressive of all languages. Attempts to write music in it, or to sing it, as if it were Italian or German or French or Russian or

Yiddish (and I've heard every one of these tried) are bound to failure" (15). But any verbal prosody will do about as well as any other, when the comparison is to a nonverbal prosody like that of music. My concern here is not the range and variety of verbal prosodies, and/or the differences between and among them, but simply the difference between all words and all music. English being the language of this book, and the language I know best, it seems to me the obvious choice.

Traditional English prosody, which on this side of the Atlantic was employed by most poets before Walt Whitman and, across the ocean, by most poets before Gerard Manley Hopkins, is founded on what I call the Chaucerian compromise. Our original English prosody, developed for the early form of the language known either as Old English or Anglo-Saxon (the terms are identical), is the prosody of *Beowulf* and other surviving poems of the eighth, ninth, and tenth centuries A.D. That primal English prosody is exclusively accentual, usually featuring a poetic line of four stresses in which only the stressed syllables count or are counted. There can be as many or as few unaccented syllables as the poet wants to use; it does not matter how many there may be. Rhyme is scarce and pretty much ornamental. What holds the Old English poetic line together, in addition to its basic four stresses, is the additional fact that two and sometimes three (but never all four) of those stresses also alliterate with one another. "Children wish they could choose their food" is a reasonable facsimile of an Old English line; so too is "Men are meant to mind their business," or "Well now I'll be damned if I'll do what I'm told." A synthetic facsimile of the Old English line, half exhibiting, half hiding its alliteration, is "Ladies are always losing gloves."

Accentual prosody is natural to a stress-phonemic language, just as syllable-counting prosodies are to non-stress-phonemic languages—leaving aside languages like Chinese, which are neither stress-phonemic nor non-stress-phonemic, but tonal. (I have no wish to tackle the dispute here, but just how truly quantitative the classical languages were is uncertain. Our grip on the prosodies of classical Latin and, especially, classical Greek is very shaky: native informants who can give us reliable information are unfortunately scarce.) A stress-phonemic language, in a nutshell, is one in which changes in stress produce changes in meaning. English is stress phonemic because if we say "con*tent*" we are saying something very different from "*con*tent." French is not stress phonemic because however we accent a word its meaning remains the same. To quote Virgil Thomson yet again—his book, *Music with Words*, is quite simply invaluable—setting verbal texts to music "is largely a matter of not disturbing the fixed elements" of the particular language (9).

Among the most fundamental considerations for prosody is the manner in which speakers of a given language utter its syllables. In non-stress-phonemic languages like French or Italian, the relative unimportance of stress results in a more or less uniform production of syllables. That is, at whatever speed a speaker of French or Italian happens to be speaking, he will produce a more or less constant number of syllables over a particular period of time. Further (and this is very significant for music), because his manner of syllable production is so uniform, the speaker of French or Italian will not drastically alter or deform the way in which particular syllables are pronounced, no matter at what speed he may be speaking. On the other hand, in stress-phonemic languages like English, the high importance of stress results in articulative differences in the manner in which both stressed and unstressed syllables tend to be pronounced, as well as in the degree of uniformity of their production. Unstressed syllables in languages like English tend to be scanted—spoken at greater speeds and with large changes in articulation, which of course also means much more variation in ready intelligibility. Since singing itself tends to stretch and deform language, it is not surprising that syllable-timed languages like French and Italian usually seem more inherently musical than stress-timed languages like English. Virgil Thomson says it best: "Serious opera seems never to have felt quite comfortable . . . in English . . ." (51). (Thomson was himself, for better or worse, the composer of several serious operas with English-language libretti; two of his libretti were written by Gertrude Stein.)

Old English, like Old England, suffered the Norman invasion of 1066. The "official" language of the country—at least as far as society, and business, and the law courts, and of course high culture as well—became and for roughly three hundred years remained Norman French. Common folk spoke English. But when military and political developments forced the invaders to choose between their newer (and secure) English domains and their ancient (and disputed) domains in France, they chose England—and also chose English. One of Geoffrey Chaucer's contemporaries, John Gower (his name can be pronounced to rhyme either with "hour" or with "more"), began his poetic career, in the latter part of the fourteenth century, by writing in French. He then wrote poetry in the safe, universal medieval tongue, Latin. And finally, as English became once again the dominant tongue in England, Gower finished his career by writing in that language. Chaucer stuck to English: the consolidations he effected proved enormously important—none less so than his magnificent (though not pioneering) demonstrations of the prosody that came to rule English poetry for five hundred years. (Despite rumors to the contrary, that prosody is still not dead and buried.) In his poetry, English prosody kept its unchangeable emphasis on stress, since the language of course remained stress-phonemic, but adapted itself to certain French characteristics. What happened, essentially, is that English prosody settled into a mode in which a poetic line was regulated by a constant number of what metricists call "feet." (A foot, briefly, is a stressed syllable plus any unstressed syllable or syllables associated with it. There can be no foot without a stressed syllable, though the total number of syllables in any given foot varies.) This sort of compromise arrangement, incorporating both the stress aspect of Old English and the syllable-counting aspect of French, may look like just another kind of syllable counting— but that's not at all what it is. An English hexameter line (that is, a line of six poetic feet) will have roughly the same number of syllables—twelve—as the standard French alexandrine. But the crucial difference is that the English line is further divided into a regular number of subentities (i.e., feet, which as I've said are not primarily organized by syllables but by stress). The French alexandrine is not so divided: the syllable truly is its basic as well as its only prosodic measure. Indeed, one powerful and little-understood feature of traditional English prosody is the pull, the tension back and forth between the native element of stress (which we can also think of as the language's natural or speech rhythm) and the foreign element of syllable counting. As I suggested in chapter 1, in castigating Joyce Kilmer's poem "Trees," it is the metrical *ir*regularities introduced by a truly fine poet, as he leans his verse out away from, but never entirely free of, the syllable-count frame, that make for genuine poetic musicality.

Let me emphasize, again, that the Chaucerian compromise was not invented by Chaucer. However, he represents its first great peak: his is the first English poetry after the Norman Conquest to fully, profoundly, and very beautifully absorb and balance out competing native English and foreign influences. This blended prosody also reduced alliteration, so important in Old English poetry, to a largely ornamental role, and elevated rhyme—so unimportant in Old English poetry, but a mainspring of French— to much more basic status. (Still, the high incidence of blank verse, which is iambic pentameter without rhyme, is a singular fact in English poetry, and markedly absent in French. John Milton's *Paradise Lost*, composed in blank verse, also features an angry prefatory denunciation of "the troublesome and modern bondage of Riming," which, Milton declaims, is "no necessary Adjunct or true Ornament of Poem or good Verse, . . . but the Invention of a barbarous Age, to set off wretched matter and lame Meter.") The use of syllable counting, plus the new emphasis on rhyme, also allowed English poetry to make use of all the replicative forms developed in Continental poetry, forms that are foreign to the Old English verse of *Beowulf* and its time.

As I have noted, the Chaucerian compromise ruled almost unchallenged for close to five hundred years. (Until recently, the challenge thrown down by William Blake in the late eighteenth century was regarded as a personal eccentricity rather than a serious divergence from established standards. In any case, Blake was far out of the mainstream of English verse and everything he did was thought aberrant; at the time he attracted little or no following.) In the second half of the nineteenth century, the American Walt Whitman, and later the Englishman Gerard Manley Hopkins, launched nontraditional prosodies that, though they initially seemed fearfully radical, have turned out to be basically retrogressive, more of a turning back toward the Old English than truly new developments. The nontraditional prosody pioneered by Whitman and Hopkins is of course no more monolithic than traditional prosody. Its chief feature, for our purposes, is the sharply reduced importance of unstressed syllables, the elimination of syllable counting, and indeed pretty much the abandonment of all regularity of either stresses or syllables. This makes nontraditional poetry much more like prose in its rhythms; it also largely does away with rhyme, at least as a fundamental, structural principle, and also eliminates the regular, replicative forms—ballads, couplets, sonnets, and the like—used in traditional verse. All of this has high significance for the musical setting of such texts.

Although there are some similarities between verbal prosodies and those of music, there are basic and very important differences. In the narrow, time-beating metrical sense, musical prosody is distinctly like that of poetry. But just as practitioners of traditional English prosody work best when they stand teetering on the narrow ledge between adhering to and breaking away from prosodic rules, so too the actualized *rhythm* of music—as opposed, that is, to the organizational *meter* of music—always bends off in its own directions. Paul Hindemith explains:

> But there is another form of musical time whose effects are quite different from those of normal time or of musical time as expressed in metrical successions. Here, in contrast to meter, *irregularity in duration is the essential condition.* . . . We can understand this dissimilarity by comparing our everyday actions as a series of temporally irrational successions of time intervals with the metrically organized time intervals as measured by watches, clocks, and other time-dividing devices. In musical time, as expressed in rhythmical forms, the time interval . . . contains many rhythmical beats which, although they can be measured by [metrical] beats, have just as little in common with them as have our temporally irrational actions with the clock's ticking. To understand such a succession as a rhythmic structure and not merely as a metrically organized row, we have to wait until it reaches its end. Then the complete form will appear to our analyzing mind as a new unit and not, as it appeared in meter, as an accumulation of single units. *All the nonmetrical constituent parts of this new unit . . . have now lost their individual meaning, and are nothing but subordinate parts of the new entity.* . . . We may say that *musical*

> *time . . . [thus] produced an effect which in normal time is nonexistent.* (59–60; emphasis added)

Hindemith's argument is not easy to grasp, especially on one reading, and perhaps even after several. What he is saying is that merely organizational measurements of music (three-fourths time, six-eighths time, and so on) are insufficiently descriptive of what actually happens to time in a piece of music—that is, in actualized music, for music that exists solely in score is no more actualized than an unread book or an unscreened movie. In a very real sense, therefore, performed music creates its own time, in which the divisions are necessarily irregular (and will in fact vary from performance to performance) and the overall effect is more like the subjective sense of time we perceive internally than it is like the time of a ticking clock. Or as Hindemith also puts it, "the sensations of musical time and musical space are not identical with time and space as felt in our everyday life or in the aesthetic effects of nonmusical works of art" (58).

This is a large but a demonstrably true assertion, though I believe that the stretching and compressing of time in the experience of nonmusical art is very comparable to what we experience in listening to music. Even though the phenomena of nonmusical art may not seem to exist in time, artistic time is far more than simple external phenomena: it exists in inner worlds as well as in outer ones. We all know the sensation of watching a film, being absorbed into its movement, and then being startled back into a perception of that other reality we call the world when the lights in the theater go back on and we find ourselves slowly and somewhat dazedly filing out to the street. Much the same thing happens when we are deeply drawn into a book, or into a piece of music: the linearity of metrical time, of clock time, is suspended and we exist, instead, by the time frame created in the book, the movie, the music. But this too is genuine time, not mere fantasy, not some imaginary, transient bubble that will be blown away when the book, the movie, or the music come to an end. While we exist in that other time, indeed, it is the only time we know. The time frame of art, while we are subject to its grip, and also, though to a lesser extent, even after that grip becomes less immediate and therefore less forceful, is also real—as real, though differently real, as the everyday reality we experience as we walk the streets or do other workaday things. Each of these different realities supersedes and thus replaces the other. As the musical theorist Victor Zuckerkandl says, using "rhythm" in the sense in which Hindemith too employs it, and using "time" to mean regular or metrical time: " 'Time' and rhythm . . . appear even to exclude each other: rhythm resists regular time; 'time' appears to suffocate rhythm" (159). And Zuckerkandl goes on to speak in terms identical to those I used, earlier, in referring to the tensions, in traditional English prosody, between natural or speech rhythm and metrical regularity:

> Confinement to the strict rule did not destroy rhythm but [eventually] led to the evolution of a completely new rhythm—rhythm bound to the law of meter, which finally proved to be nowise inferior in subtlety and power to the effect of free rhythm. And it is not rhythm despite meter, but, on the contrary, rhythm from meter, rhythm fed by forces dammed up in meter. (160)

The shifting terminology should not be allowed to confuse us. Zuckerkandl and Hindemith are in absolute agreement. Each maintains that music has two kinds of time, one regular, one irregular, and that much of the power of music stems from the playing off of one kind against the other. Zuckerkandl's "rhythm fed by forces dammed up in meter" is identical to Hindemith's "musical time, as expressed in rhythmical forms." Hindemith emphasizes that, to use a metaphor he does not employ, the microcosm belongs to meter, the macrocosm to rhythm. Too much change in the small-sized patterns of which meter is composed causes us to

> lose all feeling for metrical order; . . . the metric successions reach a critical point beyond which no meter whatever can be felt, but the feeling of the unrestrained power of free rhythm enters. On the other hand, free rhythmic forms can just as suddenly become metrified by the introduction of the slightest degree of regular temporal recurrence. (Mellers, *Music in the Making*, 87)

When Wilfrid Mellers defines the forms of music as "the means whereby composers have organized in terms of time the aural relations between tension and relaxation" (11), he too employs concepts closely parallel to those used in traditional prosody. But especially in practice, the gap between "tension and relaxation" in music is a great deal wider than the gap between speech rhythms and metrical rhythms. Zuckerkandl, after discussing many specific examples (and using excerpts from musical scores), concludes that

> in music, we never have to do with a mere sequence in time. The temporal succession here is revealed not simply as a progression but as a combination of progression and recurrence; *it does not represent itself to us in the image of a straight line but in the image of a wave.* . . . As the tones fall on the different phases and fractional phases of the wave, the variously directed kinetic impulses of the different phases successively impart themselves to the tones. . . . When we identify the beat, the part of a measure upon which a particular tone falls, we do not do so because we had secretly counted along, or reckoned up in memory, but *because the characteristic direction of the wave phase upon which the tone falls becomes directly perceptible in the tone*, can be heard in and from the tone directly, *just like any of its other qualities.* (173; emphasis added)

No such statement can be made about poetry: no matter what the metrical pattern being employed, no human ear can possibly distinguish which sequential foot in a line of poetry is being heard. Indeed, it is virtually impossible to aurally distinguish a poetic line—that is, to know while listening to poetry recited or read aloud, rather than reading it from the printed page, just where a poetic line starts and where it stops—unless we have some external marker (like the predictable placing of a rhyme) or can force ourselves to listen so mechanically that the poetic feet can be counted.

But Zuckerkandl goes still further:

> Nothing happens from tone to tone save one thing: time elapses. The mere fact of the temporal succession of the

tones, and nothing else, must produce the distinction between to and fro: the pendulum motion, the wave, must be
the work of the mere lapse of time. The wave is not an
event *in* time but an event *of* time. Time happens; time is
an event.

Thus the musician . . . is led to conclude . . . [that]
change does not create [musical] time; [musical] time
literally creates change. (185)

Plainly, for all their historically intertwined associations, music
and literature are in their very essence remarkably different.

But in fact the essence of music is even less like that of literature
than the discussion thus far would indicate. In the interests of
clarity and relative simplicity, I have been speaking of music, so
far, as if it were simply a succession of single notes, just as poetry
or prose is a succession of single words. But it is time to admit, at
long last, that music can (and frequently does) consist of two or
more—often *many* more—notes played simultaneously, a procedure that results in what we call harmony. We need also to confess
that harmony in and of itself produces highly significant effects.
And from these two facts alone, we can see that the composer's
palette extends in vastly different directions from the poet's. But
in truth it is not only harmony the composer can call on: if this
multiplicity of notes is played on different instruments, there is
instrumental tone color to take into account. Further: if notes are
played by one instrument at one dynamic level, and by another at
a different dynamic level, we have still another element to deal
with. And if we even so much as begin to face up to the possibilities
of counterpoint—one instrument or group of instruments playing
against another instrument or group of instruments—we are over-
whelmed by the ineluctable fact that, as we knew all along, music
is most definitely not poetry and poetry is not music. (I need not
mention, but as a poet and frustrated musician feel obliged to
remind you, that a single instrument, the piano, can do all of these
things at the same time—and more.)

Equally plainly, to set words to music is to do a great deal more
than simply to transpose verbal forms into musical ones—as if
that sort of translation were ever simple. I'm sure it is true, as

Robert Starer notes, that "singers have often told me that the words help them remember the musical continuity" (164). But where does the musical continuity come from, and how closely is it shaped by the words? "Anything can be set to music," says Virgil Thomson bluntly (32)—and this too is surely true, just as anything can be versified, or turned into a movie, or into a story or a novel. But set *well* to music? Mozart dealt with that problem almost daily, and in a 1781 letter to his father makes his feelings extremely clear:

> Why, an opera is sure of success when the plot is well worked out, the words written solely for the music and not shoved in here and there to suit some miserable rhyme . . . —I mean, words or even entire verses which ruin the composer's whole idea. Verses are indeed the most indispensable element for music—but rhymes—solely for the sake of rhyming—the most detrimental. (184)

Not long before, Mozart assured his father that his new opera, *Abduction from the Seraglio*, was being revised both in words and in music. Speaking of a new aria being written for the character Osmin, Mozart says: "I have explained to [Herr] Stephanie [his librettist] the words I require for this aria—indeed I had finished composing most of the music for it before Stephanie knew anything whatever about it" (181).

The twentieth-century composer Mario Castelnuovo-Tedesco, who has demonstrated an unusual fondness for setting texts to music, has spoken very plainly. "One cannot set . . . the sonnet," he insists, noting that the form

> is most unadaptable to music—first, because of the content, which is often too philosophical and intellectual; next, because of its almost too strict a form; and finally, because of the difficulty of balancing quatrains and tercets into different musical periods. The less strict forms of the *canzone* [meaning pretty much 'lyric poem'] and the *ballata* ['ballads'] are generally preferable, or poems that are entirely free. (305–6)

Not surprisingly, that devout worshiper of all free forms, Richard Wagner, strongly agrees. In a March 1854 letter to Franz Liszt he exclaims:

> I could not at any price write a melody to Schiller's verses, which are entirely intended for reading. These verses must be treated musically in a certain arbitrary manner, and that arbitrary manner, as it does not bring about a real flow of melody, leads us to harmonic excesses and violent efforts to produce artificial wavelets in the unmelodic fountain. (vol. 2, 15)

Why composers strongly prefer to set original rather than translated texts is another matter entirely, and one about which I can only say, here (for the subject is an immense one), that most composers believe translated words are also badly or weakly written words, and that no questions of verbal integrity occur when they work only with original-language texts. But composers' objections to formal or traditional poetry, and their decided preference for looser and freer forms, are only superficially parallel to poetry's own disputes about traditional versus nontraditional prosodies. A brief consideration of the translation of literary texts will help explain why this superficially attractive parallel cannot be pressed very far. Taking a twelfth-century French poem, for example, written in deeply traditional patterns, and turning it into twentieth-century English verse, is the very farthest thing from a simple transposition. I have myself translated Chrétien de Troyes's seven-thousand-line poem *Yvain*, written about 1170, so I speak from fairly intensive experience. Mere linguistic translation is totally inadequate, because the original is eight hundred years old. It has a literary form, a literary style, and follows literary and other conventions perfectly suited to a basically aristocratic twelfth-century French audience. But the modern reader of an English translation is likely not to know a word of contemporary French, much less that of the twelfth century; probably has no knowledge of and about as much interest in the literary habits of twelfth-century France; knows virtually nothing of court life at any period; and has very little idea how life was lived in the twelfth century, by what standards and according to what values. Simple transposition indeed!

But multiple and complex as are the elements to be dealt with in such a purely verbal translation, they at least all exist on the same plane—that is, in the world where words are spoken and understood. Music no more lives in that world than do those born incurably deaf and mute. So far as I am aware, there is no intelligent life on Mars, nor ever has been. But if we can imagine a twelfth-century Martian civilization, involving creatures totally alien to anything ever seen or heard on earth (or indeed on Mars itself, by the time of this twentieth century of ours), and then imagine a courtly poem, or whatever might pass for a courtly poem (or a poem at all) in that alien culture and on that alien planet, and then try to imagine translating *that* into twentieth-century English verse, I suspect we would have a much closer idea of the fundamental differences between musical and verbal modes of thought. For at bottom musically based thought is every bit as unlike verbally based thought as words themselves are unlike the mathematical flights of an Albert Einstein, according to Einstein's own understanding of his mind's operating procedures. We are fortunate to have an account written by him, in response to a psychologist's query as to "what internal or mental images, what kind of 'internal word'" he employed when trying to work out scientific problems. Einstein replied, with great care:

> The words or the language, as they are written or spoken, do not seem to play any role in my mechanism of thought. The psychical entities which seem to serve as elements in thought are certain signs and more or less clear images which can be "voluntarily" reproduced and combined.
>
> There is, of course, a certain connection between those elements and relevant logical concepts. It is also clear that the desire to arrive finally at logically connected concepts is the emotional basis of this rather vague play with the above-mentioned elements. But taken from a psychological viewpoint, this combinatory play seems to be the essential feature in productive thought—before there is any connection with logical construction in words or other kinds of signs which can be communicated to others.

The above-mentioned elements are, in my case, of visual and some of muscular type. Conventional words or other signs have to be sought for laboriously only in a secondary stage, when the mentioned associative play is sufficiently established and can be reproduced at will.

According to what has been said, the play with the mentioned elements is aimed to be analogous to certain logical connections one is searching for. (Ghiselin, 43)

Igor Stravinsky provides us with an express musical linkage to Einstein's explanation. Asked if he regarded "musical form as in some degree mathematical," he replied:

It is at any rate far closer to mathematics than to literature—not perhaps to mathematics itself, but certainly to something like mathematical thinking and mathematical relationships. (How misleading are all literary descriptions of musical form!) I am not saying that composers think in equations or charts of numbers, nor are those things more able to symbolize music. But the way composers think, the way I think, is, it seems to me, not very different from mathematical thinking. . . . Musical form is mathematical because it is ideal, and form is always ideal. (Stravinsky, *Conversations*, 34)

Stravinsky also said, in the course of the same recorded conversation, that "when I compose something, I cannot conceive that it should fail to be recognized for what it is, and understood. I use the language of music, and my statement in my grammar will be clear to the musician who has followed music up to where my contemporaries and I have brought it" (Stravinsky, *Conversations*, 32). You can perhaps have a better sense of what is meant if you recall what it was like the first time you tried to speak another language, in another country, and discovered with dismay how terribly poorly prepared you were to understand what the dullest native clod and the smallest native child could comprehend with ease. But that metaphor too does not do justice to the differences between verbal and musical language. Imagine yourself delivering with a straight face the following statement, once made by the contemporary composer Elliott Carter, if you happen, as I do, not to be a musician:

> Music is the only world in which you can really manipulate the flow of time in a rather free way. For whereas a painter is dealing with a flat, static surface, the musician is working with a constantly flowing stream of sound—so that how you make the stream flow and what obstacles you put in to stop it from flowing or to modify the flow, and so on, become fundamental, and this is what I'm trying to deal with. (37)

Carter's formulation makes me, at least, feel much the way I felt when my second son turned out to be distinctly nonverbal. Verbality being the name of my game, I of course assumed he was a bit slow, and reconciled myself to a situation I could do little about. And then, one day when he was three or four, I came into his room and found him with his back toward me, swinging back and forth, in a slow, regular rhythm, from one foot to the next. I watched for some minutes, trying to figure out what was going on. But finally I interrupted and asked what on earth he was doing. As he turned to answer, one hand raised to stop further questions, I could see that he was facing a small electric clock. "Sssh, Daddy," he said urgently. "I'm counting by fives. I'm up to 3,760." With which cogent and quite sufficient explanation he at once turned back, so as not to miss a single precious five-second marker. And I turned away, slightly dazed, having been suddenly but very fully alerted that this was a mind working in very different ways from mine, but working very agilely indeed. (At age seven, not surprisingly, he refused to play chess with me any longer, because, he explained, I could not play up to his standard. And I couldn't, he was quite right.)

Like the nonverbal thought of an Albert Einstein, musical thinking is in fact just that different from verbally based thinking. The creative process is largely identical for all members of our species, but the vehicle that carries and expresses what our minds create necessarily varies from field to field. The physicist may think spatially, the musician rhythmically, the poet verbally, and the painter in terms of color or design. It is easy to confuse the vehicle with the process and declare that every field has its own unique "inspiration." But it is just as easy to argue overforcefully that all aspects of creativity are identical, for all humans in all areas of activity. Neither position seems to me viable. The situation can perhaps be analogized to that of the relationships of hardware and software in computer use. All users need the basic central processing unit, but each substantive application requires its own specially designed software.

When a composer leaves his primary world, the universe of sound and rhythm, of pitch and dynamics and time relationships, in order to rummage about in the world he shares with the rest of us, there to search out and find a verbal text, and then proceeds back into his musical world, bringing that text with him, it being a text that he will then set to music, has he truly crossed an almost unfathomable boundary line? Is he attempting a task so full of ramifying theoretical difficulties that philosophers are likely to spend the rest of man's remaining years on earth trying to figure them out?

Take an extreme but wonderfully representative case, that of Wolfgang Amadeus Mozart. To those of his contemporaries who had heard any of his staggeringly brilliant compositions—concertos, symphonies, piano sonatas, operas, serenades, string quartets: they poured out of him like water over a dam—there seemed a strange, unaccountable gulf between the soaring music and the not terribly impressive man. Those who expected, naïvely, that music and musician would be one and the same, that there would be a complete identity between what could be found in the man's music and in the man's life and personality, even in his words and actions, were almost inevitably disappointed. His scatalogical letters, stuffed with nonsense rhymes of no great wit, are legendary. And as the musicologist Eric Blom emphasizes, literary references are almost as rare as hen's teeth in Mozart's extensive correspondence. "Here," says Blom, commenting on a brief letter to Mozart's sister, "is a very rare indication that Mozart ever read anything or took the slightest interest in literature." And Blom quickly explains that an interest in literature may not be involved, even here, for the French book in question may have been of interest to Mozart "merely in order to practise his French" (Mozart, *Letters*, 17).

Nor are we dealing simply with different levels of maturity and sophistication in different spheres of life. Mozart's life was music: everything else was secondary. When his first son was coming into the world, Mozart sat in the next room, writing the second, in D minor, of the six magnificent string quartets dedicated to Joseph Haydn. Eric Blom calls this "extraordinary emotional detachment" (Mozart, *Letters*, 212), but is it in fact extraordinary for a man who could stroll in the garden, after dinner, his hands folded behind him, his face turned unseeingly to the ground, and finally come into the house with two or three movements of a symphony fully written and scored in his head? Is it extraordinary for a small boy who, having been given lessons on the piano and having shown unmistakable signs of high musical ability of all sorts, proceeded to ask at age five or six to be allowed to watch his father and friends play chamber music, and then, the next week, further asked to be allowed to actually play with the adults? To his astonished and censorious father, Mozart explained that he did not need lessons to play second violin: he had been watching the adults, and as a result could play the instrument perfectly well. And he could: his astonished father handed him a violin and Mozart could indeed play it, never having touched one before in his life.

I spoke of trade-offs, in chapter 1, referring to the kinds of gains and losses with which the creative mind must come to terms. One such inevitable balancing has to do with the inability of the mere human—and Mozart for all his genius was in the end merely human, like all the rest of us—to operate at the same level on all the planes of his existence at the same time. The greatest innovators in any and all fields are masterful only in a very few directions, even in their central endeavors. Einstein was in fact not a terribly good mathematician. Walt Whitman, arguably the greatest prosodic innovator in the history of poetry, was distinctly derivative in his rhetoric and not radically innovative in his handling of literary form. Emily Dickinson, rhetorically as innovative as any poet who has ever lived, for the most part followed traditional forms and meters. Pablo Picasso, with a sense of line as starkly coruscating as any painter known to me, was not remarkably brilliant, though he certainly was adequate, as a colorist. Matisse, though far more innovative as a colorist, was nowhere near Picasso's equal in matters of line. Vincent van Gogh, a fantastic colorist, deliberately sacrificed issues of line; indeed, his early sketches show a dutiful, uninspired, competent but never exciting handling of line. Great athletes are virtually never great in more than one sport: when we find a Bo Jackson who can compete at the very highest level in two sports, we are stunned. How many Bo Jacksons are there? And how many of them excel in three sports? Or, in matters literary, how many major novelists, in the entire canon of English and American literature, are equally renowned as poets? That is a question I have been thinking about for years, and the only name I can think of is Thomas Hardy. As I said in chapter 1, we are "finite, mortal, intensely fallible creatures who . . . cannot comprehend how all things connect to all other things, cannot perceive even the fragmented, limited nature of our [own] perceptions."

5

LITERATURE AND MUSIC (CONTINUED)

One way of summarizing chapter 4, in words of a very few syllables, might be to say that literature and music, though intimately allied, though allies of a closeness and intimacy almost unparalleled in cultural history, are nevertheless extraordinarily unlike in their most basic natures. Music and words are so very different, indeed, that there are a good many composers who do not set texts at all; some of them admit frankly and freely that their professional relationship with verbal language seems to them inadequate, even troubling. Elliott Carter declares quite bluntly that "it is difficult to find a text that I would like to set to music," adding that he has in hand "a rather large and expensive commission" for just such a task but doubts he'll ever fulfill it—or that he wants to, "partly because I find that the speed of presentation in words is very different from the speed of presentation in my music. Also, I don't understand words very well when they're sung," he confesses, "which is a troublesome problem." And he concludes, with some vexation: "It seems to me that vocal music in general has to be rethought completely and that I don't have the time or patience to do that single-handedly" (106). That kind of separation of words and music might not have been possible, a few centuries earlier—or even a century earlier, when Richard Wagner, Giuseppe Verdi, and Giacomo Puccini bestrode the musical scene like the colossi they were. But in our time a good many arts have retreated (or been driven: that is the subject of a whole different set of lectures) into their more or less private domains. Elliott Carter's attitude can be readily paralleled among poets and novelists, among painters and sculptors, and sometimes even among such traditionally social artistic practitioners as architects and dancers.

And when the artist is ensconced in (or driven into) his private cave, he is quite likely to throw stones at anyone who tries to enter—or, at least, to argue, willy-nilly, that his cave belongs exclusively to him and, further, that there is no cave anywhere on the earth that even vaguely resembles it or is anywhere near as good. Musicians and poets once worked in relatively equal balance: neither ruled, each respected the domain and prerogatives of the other. This working balance has been seriously disturbed, in this as in many humanistic areas, and the question uppermost in both parties' minds is often: Just who's in charge around here? Is he working for me, or am I working for him? (Political infighting reaches its deadliest peak, of course, the less there is to fight over. I have never seen invective to match that flung back and forth, in the 1940s, between two splinter groups of Communists, the Trotskyites and the Schachtmanites—not to mention the vile and violent political obscenities hurled between Communist True Believers and both sets of besplintered and besplattered heretics.)

To some extent, of course, this struggle for the upper hand is also an unavoidable part of human nature itself. In any nominally equal relationship between disparate elements—one can think of the tensions between and among Congress, the President, and the Supreme Court; one can also think of the institution of marriage— the question of supremacy inevitably arises. As Lewis Carroll reminded us, in chapter 1, "The question is, which is to be master." Accordingly, one of the underlying issues of perpetual concern to almost all composers who even consider setting a text is: Which comes first, the words or the music? Even in strictly chronological terms, as Mozart makes clear, the answer is never simple, though for the most part it is the words that are first written. But the relationship between a verbal text and the music provided for that text is neither stable nor predictable, nor is the one language (verbal or musical) *necessarily* superior to the other. Sir Arthur Sullivan employed preexistent texts, but always sought to find which musical rhythm worked best before he even thought of constructing a melody, much less an orchestral accompaniment. "If I feel that I cannot get the accent right in any other way," he explained, "I mark out the [musical] metre in dits and dashes, and it is only after I have decided the [musical] rhythm that I proceed to notation" (Kolodin, 287). Richard Strauss was more demanding. Writing to his librettist, Hugo von Hofmannsthal, on 26 June 1909, he notes that "for the end of Act III" of *Der Rosenkavalier*, which he was just then beginning to compose, "I have a very pretty tune. Could you possibly write me some 12 to 16 lines in the following rhythm." Strauss then appends a marked-up poetic text, and adds, "Can't think of anything better at the moment: it's the rhythm that matters. Some such popular vaudeville poem: about 3 verses, 12 lines. On the above pattern!" (35–36) Hofmannsthal did not write the addition until almost a year later, at which time he remarked: "In the final duet . . . I was obviously very much tied down by the metre scheme which you prescribed for me, but in the end I found it rather agreeable to be bound in this way to a given tune. . . ." Four days later, he asks, pointedly, "Let me know whether the final words really do fit perfectly the closing tune you had in mind?" Strauss replied, casually, "seems perfect to me" (57–59).

Working not only with material out of another mode of thought, but also with words written by someone else, is to be sure a significant part of the composer's difficulty; it is for that reason that literary-minded musicians like Wagner and Berlioz and others have written their own texts. It is perhaps somewhat misleading to refer to my own attempts at musical composition, since I am decidedly *not* a composer and, for better or worse, I *am* a poet. But I have at least tried to operate as both a musician and a writer, so my experience is perhaps of some interest. And whenever I attempted to set a text, it was without exception my own text I set—and usually I wrote text and music simultaneously, and for a very specific circumstance or vocal-instrumental combination. (Again, it may well be that I was not drawn to the musical possibilities of other men's words because I am a pretty poor excuse for a composer; to that extent, my experience may be quite irrelevant.) The composition I best remember (all have long since been burned, so memory is all I have to guide me) was for contralto voice and B-flat clarinet: I was at the time married to the contralto voice and myself played the clarinet. The words were simplicity itself; as I noted, they evolved totally in conjunction with the music. The piece began, as I recall, something like this: "Slow now creep we, down to the water's edge, now creep we, now creep we, down." (Tennyson is said to have growled, seeing what composers had done with his poems, "Why do these damned musicians make me say a thing twice when I said it only once?" The answer should have been: Because, Lord Alfred, music is not poetry, and poetry is not music, and what requires emphasis in one art is not always what requires it in the other. And it could also have been added: Remember, too, oh noble Poet Laureate, that the poet did not write the finished song, but only the original poetic text from which the song was later made.) Neither Shakespeare nor Ira Gershwin need feel in the least threatened by my lyric. But the words did fit the music rather well: this may be the only musical composition I half regret destroying.

The composer Max Reger gets at another aspect of this whole question of literary versus musical supremacy. His wife records:

> When Reger felt the urge to write *Lieder* [songs], he would turn to me and say: "Find me some texts, dear!" Then I would go and fetch my Goethe. If then I read a poem to him or put it on his desk, he would say: "Wonderful—but this tells us everything already, what can I possibly add in my composition? . . . I find Goethe's poems so perfect that nothing more can be said about them." But often, when Reger read a little poem that others thought insignificant, a melody would suddenly come to him and he would write it down, making out of the union of the little poem and his music a perfect work of art. (Prawer, 13)

Richard Strauss says, more subtly, much the same thing. Writing to Hofmannsthal, who had indicated that he wanted his libretto to be acted out as a stage play before it was set to music as a libretto, Strauss observes that "your draft seems to me so pure and so beautifully lyrical that I don't know whether, if spoken (as opposed, that is, to being sung), it'll have anything like the effect that, as an opera, it is *bound* to have" (18). Or as Paul Hindemith neatly said: "We have tried to express that which was *not* said in one constructional element [the text] in the other [the music]—and vice versa" (13). Mario Castelnuovo-Tedesco is more effusive in his explanations, first stating the fundamental requirements for a text to be set to music and then adding his strictures:

> What is the ideal poem? Naturally, it is difficult to say. The answer depends especially upon the sensitivity of the composer, and also upon the *genre* he prefers. . . . Just the same, I believe there are some necessary conditions common to all—first, one that goes to the essence: the poem must have an "expressive core"; it should express a "state of soul," whatever the musician's preferences may cause the nature of that state to be; it should, in any case, be capable of awakening a "resonance" in the composer's soul; it should express the "core" in a perfect, simple and direct, clear, and harmonious form, rich, but without too many words. A certain "margin" should be left for the music: from this point of view, an intimate and restrained poem is preferable to a too sonorous and decorate one. . . . One cannot set "The Divine Comedy" to music. (305)

Igor Stravinsky, a much greater composer, is far more detailed about what attracts him in a poetic text. When during World War I he was reading the Russian folktales that eventually resulted in *Les Noces*, and that also underlay *L'Histoire du Soldat*—two of the most influential works of his middle period—he records in his *Autobiography* the following reactions:

> What fascinated me in this verse was not so much the stories, which were often crude, or the pictures and metaphors, always so deliciously unexpected, as the sequence of

the words and syllables, and the cadence they create, which
produces an effect on one's sensibilities very closely akin
to that of music.

Stravinsky has much more to say, and in just a moment I will let
him speak his piece. But let me interrupt him for just a moment,
to emphasize several key aspects of what he has already said. First:
he knows, specifically enumerates, and equally specifically rejects
those elements that would attract the literary mind. It is sheer
rhythm to which he is drawn. Second: it never occurs to him that
these rhythmical elements could produce any other effect than the
one they produce on him. It is almost as if James Joyce were to
look up, genuinely startled, and inquire whether it was possible
that everyone in the world didn't speak, read, and write nineteen
languages? Or if Bobby Fischer were to gape, incredulous, when
you noted that most people could not play fifty games of chess
simultaneously, while blindfolded, and quickly win all of them.
These are unmistakable signs of the artist's deep absorption in his
art.

Stravinsky continues:

> The phenomenon of music is given to us with the sole
> purpose of establishing an order in things, including, and
> particularly, the coordination between *man* and *time*. To
> be put into practice, its indispensable and single require-
> ment is construction. Construction once completed, this
> order has been attained, and there is nothing more to be
> said.

And here I must again interrupt Maestro Stravinsky, for the last
time, simply to remind you that, when he was young and terribly
sharp-tongued, he scoffed at the idea of the importance of an
orchestral conductor. What does a conductor do, after all, he
exclaimed? He fires a gun to start the piece, and then the orchestra
plays, and that's the end and sole purpose of his existence.

Stravinsky goes on:

> It is precisely this construction, this achieved order, which
> produces in us a unique emotion having nothing in com-

mon with our ordinary sensations and our responses to the impressions of daily life. One could not better define the sensation produced by music than by saying that it is identical with that evoked by contemplation of the interplay of architectural forms. Goethe thoroughly understood that when he called architecture petrified music. (*Autobiography*, 53–54)

But here I must murmur, not interrupting so much as contradicting: *au contraire.* In fact, Goethe's comment seems to me to show how little he really knew about music, just as Stravinsky's own words offer us a profound and revealing glimpse of the inside of a musician's soul, rather than explicating thoughts and sensations that nonmusicians are likely to experience. That is, Stravinsky's comparison of music and architecture tells us what *he* thinks of as being like music, rather than telling us, as words in truth cannot do, what it is really like to think musically rather than verbally. Indeed, if anything is clear by this point in our comparative examination of verbal and musical thought processes, it should be that they are largely incomparable. Like moving continents, they can meet, and even join, but they do not fuse: unlike two oceans that may come into contact, they each remain forever separate and distinct.

Given the intensity of Stravinsky's preoccupations—an intensity that should be completely understandable, though it was sometimes hard for those dealing with him to understand—it is also perfectly clear that cooperation with a man of words, on any equal basis, was impossible for him. André Gide, who did not understand this, wrote a libretto for Stravinsky to set, and the score, entitled *Persephone*, was in due time performed. Gide was horrified. He had written in his journal, before the event: "Trip to Wiesbaden, where I find Stravinsky, with whom I am to work. . . . Complete accord" (vol. 2, 167). For his part, Stravinsky thought Gide "had understood my views on the tedious subject, 'music and words.' Not that these views were difficult or obscure, or even original; Beethoven had already expressed them, in sum, in a letter to his publisher: 'Music and words are one and the same thing.' " And having gotten into the habit of annotating Stravinsky by interruption, let me point out how blandly disingenuous he is here.

Beethoven's supposed identity of music and words is very like, for Stravinsky, as if a hungry lion, smacking his lips after eating a goat, were to say that lions and goats are one and the same thing. But let me allow Stravinsky to finish:

> Words combined with music lose some of the rhythmic and sonorous relationships that obtained when they were words only. . . . They no doubt *mean* the same things; but they are magical as well as meaningful and their magic is transformed when they are combined with music. I do not say that a composer may not try to preserve or imitate effects of purely verbal relationships in music. . . . But this approach implies something of what is meant by the phrase "setting words to music," a limited pejorative description that is certainly as far from Beethoven's meaning as it is from mine.
>
> Gide understood little or nothing of all this, however; or, if he understood, disagreed. . . . He had expected the *Persephone* text to be sung with exactly the same stresses he would use to recite it. He believed my musical purpose should be to imitate or underline the verbal pattern: I would simply find pitches for the syllables, since he considered he had already composed the rhythm. . . . And not understanding that a poet and musician collaborate to produce *one* music, he was only horrified by the discrepancies between my music and his. (*Memories*, 205–6)

Again, there are important linkages between words and music, and influences moving in both directions. But neither the abundant and fruitful connections, nor the obviously generative impulses, can change the plain fact—and I trust it is by now a very plain fact indeed—that musical and verbal minds operate in very different ways. Even in dealing quite directly with literary texts, the composer inevitably transforms, and even *de*forms, the words with which he works. If he does not, if he merely provides a vapid excuse for music, more or less adorning the words but essentially leaving them as they were, we very properly say that he has done a poor job and is a poor composer. It is central to his musical task, that is, that he thus transform and even deform the nonmusical materials with which he has chosen to associate his music. We can call the process one by which the verbal text is incorporated into a new musical entity, or we can speak of verbal primacy giving way to musical primacy, or we can say that the verbal text survives, but only in an altered, transformed form. However we choose to describe what happens, the process must be a drastic one and, once again, it is an inevitable part of what a composer is up to.

But before I go any further, let me quickly spell out the true meaning, in this context, of the term "inevitable." Those who do not practice an art often find it hard to understand the idea of anything restrictive being "inevitable." Why, they ask, can't everyone at least try to write poetry like Shakespeare's and music like Beethoven's—or poetry like Milton's and music like Tchaikovsky's—or poetry like Wordsworth's and music like Dvořák's? It can seem to the nonpractitioner that artists willfully turn away from tried-and-true methodologies, struggling to find or invent newer but less attractive ones of their own. If the well-tempered fugue was good enough for Bach, why does Stravinsky have to write ragged dissonances? If Milton and Wordsworth employed smooth-flowing blank verse, who are less well-established artists to attempt anything different? But the answer is extraordinarily simple. Each and all artistic procedures and methodologies are a response to a particular time, a particular culture, and a complex of highly specific stimuli. Once that time has gone, and that culture has changed—as we know that all cultures must and do—those stimuli inevitably change too, and the artist's response, equally inevitably, has to change as well. "The attire that fashion prescribes for men of the same generation," says Igor Stravinsky, "imposes upon its wearers a particular kind of gesture, a common carriage and bearing that are conditioned by the cut of the clothes. In a like manner the musical apparel worn by an epoch leaves its stamp upon the language, and, so to speak, upon the gestures of its music, as well as upon the composer's attitude towards tonal materials" (*Poetics*, 73). The artist does not live in some never-never world of pure creation: he lives in a particular time, in a particular physical and social culture, and cannot even if he wants to escape from those completely basic and formative circumstances. Like it or not, he is shaped and stamped by the world into which he is born and in which he comes to maturity: this is an inescapable aspect of every human's life, and despite muddle-headed claims to the contrary the artist is in no way exempted. Accordingly, an artist who attempts to work in styles and with methodologies and practices developed and perhaps perfected by predecessors born into and working in a different time and different cultural circumstances is trying to do the impossible. No one can escape from inescapable constraints—and to the extent that the artist may appear to be successful, what he in fact will have escaped from is art itself. That is, because truth is an absolute requirement, the musician who writes straightforwardly Bach-like fugues, or the poet who simply apes Milton or Wordsworth's blank verse, neither is nor can be anything more than a well-schooled fraud. Truth requires that the artist be who he is and not someone else, which obviously means that there can be no truth in such a derivative pathway. And when there can be no truth, there can be no art. Pastiche and ingenious reconstruction remain only pastiche and clever but meaningless artifice. They may be pleasant to hear or read or behold; they may display much ingenuity and learning. But neither ingenuity nor learning have anything to do with truth. Not only is neither required for art, but both in fact place a heavy burden on any artist who relies on them, since by their very nature they tend to divert the artist from the particular, individual truth that he and he alone can represent. No matter how genuine the imitated originals, imitation is by definition a mere mirror reflection, a trick, a device of the intellect but without a soul of its own. As if, by wearing a frock coat or a wig, one could become a citizen of the eighteenth century! To be sure, bring Johann Sebastian Bach himself back to life and, before he has made any kind of adjustment to our new forms of existence, *he* of course could compose genuine, truthful music in Bach-like styles and forms. But even he, once he would have made the time-change—that is, once he managed to become in some sense a citizen of the twentieth century as well as of the eighteenth—would inevitably sound truly Bach-like no longer. As Robert Schumann said, "Let us be certain that were a genius like Mozart to be born today, he would write concertos in the manner of Chopin rather than in the manner of Mozart" (80).

None of this should be surprising. Is the Beethoven we see in the interesting but in good part derivative First Symphony more, in truth, than a remote ancestor of the composer of the titanic Ninth Symphony? And what is *all* artistic or human growth but the change produced by different circumstances? To be capable of such growth can indeed be defined as the ability to meaningfully respond to new and different stimuli. If you lack or are deficient in that ability, you are an immature human or—like Camille Saint-Saëns—an artist frozen at one stage of development and incapable of going any further. Just listen to the music written by Saint-Saëns in 1921 (he was born in 1835): it sounds like something rescued from a time capsule, not simply totally inappropriate but incredibly shallow. We expect a bird to sing the same song over and over—though scientists have now established that even birds change their tunes. Saint-Saëns moved on into the twentieth century, but his music did not. He was alive in 1921, but his music, once so charming and sparkling, had mummified.

In short, "inevitable" is the only right and accurate term we can use, because it precisely describes the underlying reality with which artists and nonartists alike must deal, whether they choose to or not. There is, bluntly, no volition involved. It may be hard to grasp that irreducible fact: we tend, in our time, to glamorize artists as bundles of free choice and unencumbered volition, and there are artists who love to assure us they are all that and more. But an unpalatable reality remains no less a reality than a pleasant one, and because it neither depends upon nor has any connection with our decisions and choices it must always and inevitably be confronted, like all reality, on its rather than on our terms.

And—to return to my subject—the fundamental differences between musical and literary creation are just such a reality. Mario Castelnuovo-Tedesco observes that the voice part of a song, and also the accompaniment, are "latent" in the poem. But the "expressive core" (309) of which he speaks is in truth something quite different from whatever the poet may have thought was central to his poem. And the proof, as they say, is in the pudding. Working with words, what the poet obviously produces is his poem. But working with both the poem and his own musical resources, what the musician subsequently produces is demonstrably not the poem at all, but a song, an aria, some musical production that surely has a resemblance to its verbal starting place but that is just as surely not identical to it. Nor can it be surprising, when we consider poem and musical composition in these terms, that the processes by which the poet arrives at *A* are not at all the same as the processes by which the musician arrives at *B*.

What is often called "nonliterate art"—that is, in the context of this discussion, music produced by people who are not trained in the elaborate techniques and methodologies of Western classical music—can offer useful illumination. As Wilfrid Mellers says in his fine book on the Beatles, in all rock and roll

> the word, with intellectually communicable meaning, is almost totally insignificant. . . . For Elvis Presley, Chuck Berry and the early Beatles, language was not a natural adjustment of ways to means but . . . a trigger for magical release. . . . The verses of all [Bob Dylan's] songs—and those of a Leonard Cohen, a Joni Mitchell, a Sandy Denny—re-create oral rather than literate principles of composition. (27)

Speaking of later Beatles songs, Mellers says: "The words function like runic poetry, reverberant though not intellectually formalised. . . . The point of the words lies—another inspired example of oral composition—in their opacity" (91, 104). The oral nature of the music, indeed, affects not only the words but the music too, for as Mellers notes in analyzing John Lennon's songs written just after the breakup of the Beatles, "The powerful effect of these Lennon solo songs is even more than normally misrepresented by any attempt at written notation: this is 'oral' music that can be realised only by way of oral techniques" (166). Thus, once again in Mellers's words, "to deplore the illiteracy of the Beatles . . . is nonsensical: for the essence of their achievement is that it is a return from literate and visual to aural and oral culture" (189–90).

Mellers exaggerates a bit. The very different nature of folk music, for example, includes the clear and indisputable fact that there is full permeability as between verbal and musical components. Each is not only deeply responsive to the other, but each depends upon and cannot have true existence without the other. But then, neither the words nor the music of folk song is the product of a strictly individual consciousness—at least, not in the same sense that Igor Stravinsky is the author of *Petrouchka* or William Shakespeare the author of *Macbeth*. Individuals are probably responsible for most of the folk songs we know of. In modern times there are clear examples—as for instance John Jacob Niles, here in the United States—of individuals composing folk songs that promptly achieve the status and currency of older, anonymous work. But to compose in the folk-song vein requires of the individual the surrender of most, and probably close to all, the particular, individualized approaches practiced in more learned art. Again, the proof of the pudding is in the eating: anyone who composes too successfully in the folk-song mode (as John Jacob Niles plainly did) falls quickly into the anonymous background, along with all the other composers of folk material, and in effect ceases to be able to claim such compositions as "his." Having been composed out of the stuff of the folk, they become the property of the folk. Contrariwise, a composer who employs folk devices, but does not surrender his more individual approach, can never compose directly for the folk, but only for the very different literate audience to which he himself belongs. You cannot have your cake and eat it too; put differently, there are no free lunches.

The Beatles, therefore, have not so much moved back toward oral composition as simply away from more lettered and learned composition. They have, however, used elements of both methods: the proof, yet again, is that we can and do distinguish not only authorial stances as between the Beatles and other rock-and-roll groups, like the Rolling Stones, but even as between and among the various Beatles themselves. For those who listen to the "Fabulous Four," as they were once called, such questions as who composes, who sings lead, who plays what and when, remain extremely interesting inquiries. No such possibilities exist for true oral music. We can tell Spanish folk music from that of Hungary or Japan. But we will seek in vain to make these distinctions on anything like the sort of individualized basis we can employ in dealing with the Beatles.

Let me briefly turn to literature's nonspecific, inspirational influence on music. Claude Debussy's "Prélude à l'après-midi d'un faune," a wordless orchestral composition closely based upon Mallarmé's poem "L'Après-midi d'un faune," is about as fine a turning point as one can find, as we move away from music that directly employs verbal texts and into the consideration of music less directly inspired by literature. Mallarmé's text is erotic and evocative rather than narrative and logical—exactly the sort of ideal poetic text, indeed, described by Debussy several years before he wrote his "Prélude." Speaking about a possible operatic libretto, he said that what he wanted was a poet "who only hints at what is to be said. . . . No place, nor time. No big scene. No compulsion on the musician, who must complete and give body to the work of the poet" (129). Or, in short, what he envisaged was a literary text clearly subordinate to and wholly the servant of the music. Indeed, all Debussy intended in his "Prélude," in his own words, was "a general impression of the poem." And how better to deal with a verbal text, when music is your overwhelming concern? The musical goals of the "Prélude" are elaborated more specifically by a program note accompanying one of the early performances, which note was either directly written or at the very least approved by the composer:

> The music of this *Prélude* is a very free illustration of Mallarmé's beautiful poem. By no means does it claim to be a synthesis of the latter. Rather there are the successive scenes through which pass the desires and dreams of the faun in the heat of this afternoon. Then, tired of pursuing the fearful flight of the nymphs and the naiads, he succumbs to intoxicating sleep, in which he can finally realize his dreams of possession in universal Nature. (14)

Pierre Louÿs called the "Prélude" a "delicious paraphrase" of the poem (Debussy, 141). A contemporary musician and music critic, Alfred Bruneau, declared after the "Prélude's" first public performance that Debussy "has now undertaken to explain to us symphonically the ecologue of Mr. Stéphane Mallarmé" (146). Mallarmé himself, after the first performance, wrote to Debussy that "your illustration of *L'Après-midi d'un faune* would present no dissonance with my text, unless to go further, indeed, into the nostalgia and the light, with finesse, with malaise, with richness." Hearing an earlier piano version of the score, Mallarmé had told Debussy "I was not expecting anything of this kind! This music prolongs the emotion of my poem, and sets its scene more vividly than color" (Debussy, 12, 13). (Note the significant assertion that, here, music has done still better than visual art in "depicting" the essence of a verbal text.) And Hans-Jost Frey, a Mallarmé scholar, has proposed an even closer, almost blow-by-blow correspondence of music and literary text (Debussy, 96). No such explicit matching is really possible: one is tempted to echo Erik Satie, who, asked by Debussy how he liked the first section of *La Mer*, entitled "From dawn to dusk on the waves," replied that he was particularly fond of the bit at about ten-thirty. Still, it would be hard to read the poem and listen to the music and *not* hear the resemblances.

What then was Debussy up to? What, that is, did he think he was doing, and why did he do it? What were the musical satisfactions involved in so closely matching Mallarmé's poem to his music? After all, he could have composed an orchestral piece about fauns and summer meadows and nymphs and erotic dreams, quite without reference to Mallarmé. And it would have turned out pretty much the same—or would it?

I have quoted one aspect of Pierre Louÿs's approving remarks; let me now quote him more fully. "Your *Prélude* is admirable. . . . It was not possible to make a more delicious paraphrase of *the verses that we both love*. There is always a breeze in the leaves, and so varied, so changing" (Debussy, 141; emphasis added). The key words are "the verses that we both love." Simply stated, Louÿs here recognizes, as we must too, that the process is an elemental one. Mallarmé's poem has moved Debussy so powerfully that, as a musician, his intense appreciation and affection for the literary text have resulted in his being prompted ("inspired," though I frankly do not like the word "inspiration") to create music, in part in its honor, in part to celebrate and express the feelings created in him by Mallarmé's words. (Pierre Louÿs adds, showing that his is not an unbalanced, uncritical appreciation, that "to hear your piece again I shall wait for a slightly better performance. The horns stank, and the rest were hardly better.") Musicians' feelings are as amenable to human experience and emotion as are poets', or painters', or anyone else's. As Debussy said, writing to a friendly music critic:

> The *Prélude à "L'Après-midi d'un faune,"* dear Sir, might it be what remains of the dream at the tip of the faun's

flute? More precisely, it is a general impression of the poem, for if music were to follow more closely it would run out of breath, like a dray horse competing for the Grand Prize with a thoroughbred. There is also my scorn for that eager-beaver learning that weighs down our proudest brains. And then there is no reverence for the key! Rather it is in a mode that tries to contain all the shadings, which is very logically demonstrable. Now still, all of it does follow the rising movement of the poem. And there is the scenery, marvelously described in the text, with furthermore, the humanity contributed by thirty-two violinists who had to get up too early. The end is the last line [of the poem] prolonged: *"Couple, adieu: je vais voir l'ombre que tu devins.* You two, good-bye! I'm going to see the shadows that you become."* (14)

Debussy may claim that what he has been up to is "very logically demonstrable," but he knew perfectly well that logic was not the mainspring of his work. His old teacher, Ernest Guiraud, complained in a conversation recorded about 1890: "I am not saying that what you do isn't beautiful, but it's theoretically absurd." (This is, incidentally, rather like the equally stodgy Saint-Saëns complaint that the gorgeously lush "Prélude" was deficient in formal melodic structures! For the record, Saint-Saëns also remarked, scornfully, after the first performance of César Franck's majestic Symphony in D, that "the English horn is not an instrument which solos.") Debussy's response to Guiraud was simplicity itself: "There is no theory. You have merely to listen. Pleasure is the law" (Debussy, 131). As I have over and over again said to young would-be writers, there are no laws—and if there are any, there is only one, which states: "Thou shalt not be dull."

Plainly, we are back to a consideration of creativity, this time in the musical mind. Aaron Copland has grappled wonderfully honestly with the problem:

Out of the recesses of his thought [the composer] produces, or finds himself in possession of, the generative idea. Although I say "the recesses of his thought," in actuality the source of the germinal idea is the one phase in creation that resists rational explanation. All we know is that the moment of possession is the moment of inspiration; or to use Coleridge's phrase, the moment when the creator is in "a more than usual state of emotion." Whence it comes, or in what manner it comes, or how long its duration one can never foretell. Inspiration may be a form of superconsciousness, or perhaps of subconsciousness—I wouldn't know; but I am sure it is the antithesis of self-consciousness. (52)

For many people, the artist's notion of "possession" is not immediately apprehendable. In trying to describe the creative process, Igor Stravinsky speaks of "the intuitive grasp of an unknown entity already possessed but not yet intelligible, an entity that will not take definite shape except by the action of a constantly vigilant technique" (*Poetics*, 52). "For me at least," I myself wrote twenty years ago in my first book on translation, "possession is all, incorporation, psychic ingestion, entire and whole." Trying to explain why I felt possessed of French poetry but did not feel possessed of Indonesian, though my command of the two languages and cultures was roughly equivalent, I said that "there is something in the Indonesian which remains alien, which I cannot totally ingest. And so I translate." But even this is a variable reaction, as I also noted. Indonesian lines like *Pena dan penjair keduanja mati, / Berpalingan!* always come to me in translation: "Pen and poet, both dead, / Turning!" But some Indonesian lines, like *Aku mau hidup seribu tahun lagi*, "I want to live another thousand years," remain in Indonesian in my head (160–61). I have no explanation for the difference: both sets of verses are by Indonesia's greatest poet, Chairil Anwar, and I have translated all his surviving poetry.

Robert Schumann rightly mocked the simplistic one-to-one equivalences that some people see in the creative process.

In composing his *Pastoral* Symphony Beethoven well understood the danger he incurred. His explanatory remark, "Rather expressive of the feeling than tone painting," contains an entire aesthetic system for composers. And it

> is absurd for painters to portray him sitting beside a brook, his head in his hands, listening to the bubbling water! (96)

"For in truth," Stéphane Mallarmé asked, in a lecture entitled *Music and Literature*, "what is literature if not our mind's ambition (in the form of language) to define things; to prove to the satisfaction of our soul that a natural phenomenon corresponds to our imaginative understanding of it" (Debussy, 114). Or as the philosopher Susanne Langer beautifully put it—and hers are far and away the best philosophic analyses of art I know of: "Art is the creation of forms symbolic of human feeling" (*Feeling and Form*, 40). What else is a composer like Hector Berlioz talking about when, explaining in his *Memoirs* the genesis of his symphony for viola and orchestra, *Harold in Italy*, he notes that "I decided to give it as a setting the poetic impressions recollected from my wanderings in the Abruzzi, and to make it a kind of melancholy dreamer in the style of Byron's Childe Harold" (271)? And Berlioz's ascription of the emotional tone of his music to two kinds of feelings that he has himself experienced, one while on a walking tour, the other after reading Byron, is in turn reminiscent of Paul Hindemith's portrayal of music's ability to conjure up emotions:

> Of course we know that music compensates its recipients in a manner not accessible to other arts. The range of emotions it can touch is infinitely larger, the variety within this range is unlimited, the tempo of consecutive emotions is unbelievably fast. [And] we know the reason for this: the emotions released by music are no real emotions, they are mere images of emotions that have been experienced before. . . . (57)

But Hindemith's stance is excessively as well as deliberately unromantic. In his concern to make music a functional rather than an aesthetic process—the famous *Gebrauchsmusik*, or Workaday Music, controversy from which he never escaped—he has tried to deny to music and only to music the power to deal with real feelings. "Paintings, poems, sculptures, works of architecture, after having impressed us . . . do not—contrary to music—release [only] images of feelings; instead they speak to the real, untransformed, and unmodified feelings" (57). But this is of course nonsense. Words, for example, are no more than puffs of sound, when spoken, and only bits of ink on a page, when printed. They are not the reality they purport to represent, but only symbols—or if you will, images—of that reality. "Language [certainly] gives outward experience its form, and makes it definite and clear," explains Susanne Langer. "[But] the form of language does not reflect the natural form of feeling, so that we cannot shape any extensive concepts of feeling with the help of ordinary, discursive language. . . . The real nature of feeling is something language as such—as discursive symbolism—cannot render" ("Cultural Importance," 70). The same statement can obviously be made of all the arts, including music. But as Langer also explains, "what discursive symbolism—language in its literal use—does for our awareness of things about us and our own relation to them, the arts do for our awareness of subjective reality, feeling and emotion; they give form to inward experiences and thus make them conceivable. . . . The arts objectify subjective reality, and subjectify outward experience of nature" ("Cultural Importance," 82, 84). That is, what workaday language cannot handle, poetic and other artistic language can. The arts—all the arts—can show us ourselves, bringing the dim, vague inner world into sharp, clear light. As Langer says, the arts—all the arts—"objectify subjective reality." Nor is there any other process that can accomplish this for us. "The only way we can really envisage vital movement, the stirring and growth and passage of emotion, and ultimately the whole direct sense of human life," says Langer, "is in artistic terms" ("Cultural Importance," 82).

Accordingly, those symbolic representations that constitute the arts have naturally taken on for us a status that by now is for all intents and purposes exactly parallel to, and therefore in practice essentially identical with, the *feelings* the arts symbolize. And what we are therefore led to experience, through any of the arts, has for us come to be essentially identical with the feelings and emotions themselves. We have had more than enough firsthand proof of art's truth; our trust is not an intellectual or even a conscious affair, but virtually instinctive. Who has not lifted his eyes from a book or a picture, or walked out of a concert hall, shaken by emotion?

There is much discussion, currently, about the dangerously negative power of violent pornography. For us, and perhaps even for the Cro-Magnon cave dwellers who seem to have been the first humans to bring any of the arts to perfection, sensuousness in a painting is directly and immediately perceived and experienced as sensuousness; horror in a poem is perceived and experienced as horror; erotic or violent passion in a sculpture is perceived and experienced as erotic or violent passion.

Plainly, then, music can no more be singled out and discriminated against, as Hindemith has done, than any of the other arts. All are different, to be sure; all work with different raw materials and appeal in dissimilar ways to different aspects of our senses and our minds. But all are equally, and equally effectively, representational; that is, all are equally capable of stirring completely genuine feelings. "For the listener," as the composer Roger Sessions says, music is not "an incident or an adjunct but an independent and self-sufficient medium of expression" (7).

In short, though other poets and writers may not like me to admit it, the "inspirational" effects of literature on music are of precisely the same nature as anything else that happens to affect and stir the person who happens to be a composer. To be sure, literature has powers that much of ordinary experience lacks. In particular, literature—like all art—is compressed, shaped expression. Ordinary experience usually unrolls like the child's scornful definition of history: "just one damned thing after another." But literature—again, like all art—packs as much meaningful substance into each small facet of expression as it possibly can. Just as your lover's words will have a greater effect on you than words spoken by a salesman or a clerk, so too literature simply packs a more potent punch than raw, unshaped experience. And this will sometimes mean that its power extends even more deeply into the music it engenders, affecting matters of structure as well as tonality, melody, harmony. Sibelius's biographer records, for example, that in the tone poem "The Wood-Nymph," based on a poem by Viktor Rydberg, Sibelius "strictly follows the narrative and allows it to determine the musical shape of the work" (163). Preexistent, carefully shaped literary narrative plainly has affected other composers in much the same way. But this is all simply part of that larger impact which ordered and shaped artistic experience can have. It does not change literature's basic nature or its role as only one among many, many possible formative influences. Mallarmé claimed, with his typically intense romanticism, that "Music and Literature constitute the moving facet—now looming towards obscurity, now glittering unconquerably—of that single, true phenomenon which I have called Idea" (Debussy, 115). He may have been right—but painting and sculpture and architecture deserve their places, too, and along with them, willy-nilly, love, comfort, desire, anger, frustration, ambition, and far too many emotions and provocations ever to be listed in full. Literature is a singularly important source of generative feelings for composers; it must always be remembered, however, that in this role literature is only one among a host of others. It deserves recognition; it does not deserve overstatement.

But the same cannot be said of music's influence on literature, and on poetry in particular. Prose fiction and other literary forms too are affected by music and musicians. We would not otherwise have novels like Thomas Mann's *Doctor Faustus* or the enormously potent role of a single musical phrase in Marcel Proust's *À la recherche du temps perdu*. There are some extraordinary and unusual novels, like James Joyce's *Ulysses*, as to which it might well be argued that the structural and stylistic effects of music are more significant (and more readily traced) than those of virtually any other nonliterary influence. Joyce was, after all, an intensely musical man and at one time seriously considered a career as a singer. Indeed, he made it very clear that certain parts of *Ulysses*, notably the Sirens chapter, were very consciously based on musical patterns. "I wrote this chapter," he declared, "with the technical resources of music. It is a fugue with all the musical notations: *piano, forte, rallentendo*, and so on. A quintet occurs in it, too, as in *Die Meistersinger*, my favorite Wagnerian opera" (Ellmann, 459). Although a fugue containing an operatic quintet is plainly a fugue with a difference, Joyce stuck to his guns when friends criticized the chapter. "Perhaps I ought not to say any more on the subject of the *Sirens*," he wrote, "but the passages you allude to were not intended by me as recitative. There is in the episode only one example of recitative, on page 12 in preface to the song. They are all the eight regular parts of a *fuga per canonem . . .*" (Ellmann,

461–62). Recitatives? Now, it is true, as Robert Erickson says, that "every fugue that is well made has a form, a particular shape, but no two fugues are alike, and in no sense can one think of a preexisting 'fugue form' into which all fugues can somehow be fitted. The form happens; it is a result of procedures, not a box into which the music is poured . . ." (131). But recitatives? Much more appropriately, Joyce referred to his last book, that unfortunately misbegotten misconception, *Finnegans Wake*, as "pure music" (Ellmann, 703). It may well be music, since clearly it is neither language nor literature in any usual sense of either of those words.

All the same, music's effect on prose fiction, and longer prose fiction in particular, remains necessarily less powerful and dispositive than its effect on poetry. Let me address this immense topic very briefly.

To begin with, poetry and music are historically and indissolubly linked. Our word "song," for example, can mean either a piece of music or a poem. Poets are often referred to (and just as often refer to themselves) as "singers." A poem may be criticized because it does not "sing," as a poet may be criticized because of defects in his "ear." One large subdivision of the poetic kingdom belongs to the "lyric," which is defined as verse that is "songlike." There have been entire historical periods when the two arts were regularly united in one person—as for example the period cited in Joyce's, and my own, favorite opera, Wagner's *Die Meistersinger*. There, the hinge on which the whole story turns is recognition of the tightly interwound integrity of literary text and musical expression. That joining of poet and musician in one person does not often occur, today, though Berlioz and Wagner wrote their own libretti and the librettist of Verdi's two great final operas, *Otello* and *Falstaff*, was Arrigo Boito, an accomplished composer in his own right. (His opera *Mefistofele* is still performed and is well worth listening to.) But the basic linkages can never be broken. And the poet will always seek to march his words melodically, harmoniously, trying to make them rise off the page and soar like birds—or, in an equally common metaphor, like music.

To measure some of music's impact on twentieth-century poetry's largest figures, simply consider these obvious facts:

Wallace Stevens's long-delayed and monumental first book was called *Harmonium*. Among the poems collected in it are "Sonatina to Hans Christian," "Hymn from a Watermelon Pavilion," "To the One of Fictive Music," and "Peter Quince at the Clavier." But this is only to enumerate bare titles. Among the poems without musically related titles there are lines like "their memorials are the phrases / Of idiosyncratic music"; "the trees, like serafin, and echoing hills, / That choir among themselves"; "my ears made the blowing hymns they heard"; "palms, / Squiggling like saxophones"; "These / Are the music of meet resignation"; "the still sustaining pomps / Of speech which are like music so profound"; "The mandoline is the instrument / Of a place.// Are there mandolines of western mountains? / Are there mandolines of northern moonlight?"; "In the morning, / The jack-rabbit sang to the Arkansaw"; "In the beginning, four blithe instruments / Of differing struts, four voices several"—and I have collected these random samples in minutes, simply turning a few (but nowhere near all) of the book's pages.

Ezra Pound's eight-hundred-page magnum opus, or at least what he intended as a magnum opus, was from the beginning entitled *The Cantos*.

T. S. Eliot's last major poetry was *Four Quartets*. I have argued, in my study of Eliot, that the early poem most basic to understanding the curve and arc of his career is the four-part "Preludes." I have also noted in that study, though it is a fact insufficiently appreciated, that Eliot was a sufficiently competent pianist to play the Beethoven sonatas. When he talked about music heard deeply and from the inside, accordingly, he did not speak from ignorance.

There are six poems entitled "song" in E. E. Cummings's first book, *Tulips and Chimneys*. One of the love poems in that book begins: "yours is the music for no instrument." One of the book's "post impressions" begins: "at the head of this street a gasping organ is waving moth-eaten tunes." And one of the book's "impressions" begins with a marvelously mixed synesthetic metaphor: "the sky a silver / dissonance by the correct / fingers of April / resolved."

Not every poet, to be sure, feels himself so closely connected to music. Turning the pages of Robert Frost's collected poems does not reveal much concern with music, other than a few generalized references to "song" and "singing." Robert Lowell's *Life Studies*, too, can be thumbed largely in vain, aside from a satirical reference to "my Great Aunt Sarah . . . learning *Samson and Delilah* . . . [and thundering] on the keyboard of her dummy piano." But these are on the whole the exceptions, rather than the rule, in *Life Studies*.

Not surprisingly, music's impact on my own poetry has been both large and, to me at least, important. My major acknowledgment of that influence is a book-length cycle of poems, *Beethoven in America*, that was born, about ten years ago, out of what the Elizabethans would have called a poetic conceit. Imagine, I began to wonder, what it would be like if a glorious composer like Beethoven was somehow not dead after all—if he were in fact alive and physically present in the United States—indeed, if he had materialized in my own household and become for a time my house guest. Like many poetic conceits, this one quickly took on a singularly determined life of its own. For almost a year, everyone who knew me had also to put up with Beethoven's constant presence. "Was Beethoven there?" people would inquire after a social function—and especially after a concert. For me, in truth, his presence, like his music, was so intensely real that, years later, I was forced to write one final poem, addressed directly to Beethoven, warning him to remember that his visit was over and that phase, at least, of our intimacy was done.

Let me conclude this brief discussion by setting out a poem that occurs roughly a third of the way through *Beethoven in America*. Its title is "Critics." I think that is all the introduction it needs.

> "Now that I hear them," Beethoven half whispered to
>   me, one night,
> When we had remedied history for the half-dozenth
>   time
> By playing him a superb recording of his ninth
>   symphony,
> "Now that I really and truly hear them, I admit the
>   vocal writing is rather craggy,
> Maybe even a little difficult." He smiled. "Ach, Herr
>   Raffel,
> Do you know how it hurts to admit that maybe the
>   critics were right?"
> Did I know!

"Difficult, shmifficult," I answered, "they've been
    managing for almost two hundred years.
Don't change a single note!"
He was startled. "Himmel! What an idea!
Did you think I would? After all this time? Never, I
    assure you: never."
And then I smiled too. "The difficult is good for us,
    Herr Beethoven,
Though the critics don't know it. They like the perverse,
Which is not at all the same thing."
He patted my hand and chuckled: "We have a hard time
    of it,
We artists, don't we?" I laughed with him
And then we drank to our pain and suffering
In amber Courvoisier brandy, V.S.O.

6

VISUAL ART;
PRACTICAL
RECOMMENDATIONS

Literature and music involve different processes of symbolization; their syntactical structures, too, are almost entirely different. Still, both literature and music represent methods by which we transform movement in the brain into movement in words and sounds. This shared element of transformation is fundamental, and allows for as much overlap between the two processes as in fact exists.

There is of course mental activity involved in the production of visual art, as there is also symbolization. But the syntax is sharply different: painting and sculpture involve far more representation of the actual than do either literature or music, and so, far less transformation and symbolization. It is all very well to say that a line or a three-dimensional shape is no more a line or a shape than a word is a word or than a sequence of notes is a sequence of notes. But a line or a shape has a full, complete immediacy that neither words nor notes can possibly achieve. Lines and shapes *are*; they do not need to symbolize anything in order to exist, nor do they need to be transformed. And they do not need to represent or portray anything: the actuality that they embody is their own—an actuality that is theirs by nature alone. We can speak of "found art"—that is, visual arrangements that are not created but only perceived and in a sense approved by the artist. We cannot speak of "found words" (in spite of the magnificent scene in Rabelais, where frozen words are imagined to fall onto the deck of Pantagruel's boat and thaw and become audible); neither, despite John Cage, can we speak of "found music." This difference is absolutely fundamental. It necessarily affects virtually every aspect of the painter's or the sculptor's work.

Take color, for example. The beginning student, as I vividly remember, is often denied any use of color. When color is finally permitted, its use may be sharply restricted—say, one color only, primary and not mixed, and confined to a narrowly defined maximum space. This severe rationing compels the student to weigh his choices with immense care: like a dessert-starved chocoholic permitted only one small sweet from a vast, heavily laden tray, he chooses after an almost solemn deliberation.

There are training procedures in literature and music that might be seen as roughly parallel. The aspiring poet, for example, might at first be denied access to adjectives, and then permitted just one per poem. The hopeful composer might be kept from the orchestra and confined for a time to the black-and-white of pianistic scoring. But though the training goals would indeed be parallel, the underlying realities are not. That is, to the extent that adjectives and orchestral scoring (often referred to, significantly, as orchestral "coloring") represent intensifications, and visual color can also be viewed as an intensification, there are similar pedagogical points to be made. But the purely physical fact of color is so inevitable in everything we see that, in truth, it cannot ever be truly excluded— as Kazimir Malevich demonstrated, early in this century, with canvases like his famous "White on White." The physical scientist long ago demonstrated that there is indeed no such thing as "white"—that all color is optically (one might say prismatically) of a piece—so that what we like to call "black" is not a color but the absence (or blocking) of color. The poet can perfectly well do without adjectives. The young poet in particular might not like to do without, but his poetry may be much the better for it. The musician can perfectly well do without instrumental color. Many composers actually prefer the keyboard, and some, like Stravinsky, compose only on a keyboard. (It is very common for instrumental scoring to be the last phase of a composer's work.) But shades and colors and tints and hues are never eliminated from either painting or sculpture; they may be downplayed or even distorted, but they are always and inevitably *there.*

So too with pictorial or structural composition. How else, indeed, could a photographer, who does not invent what his camera captures, possibly manage to "compose" a shot? It may not be easy to create, or to recognize, a structural composition that will interest and excite the beholder's eye, any more than it can be easy to create satisfying or exciting verbal or musical structures. But whether or not visual structures preexist, they obviously exist—and exist quite apart from anything we do or do not do. Neither the sonnet nor the symphony are in that sense natural forms. But there is nothing in a painting or a piece of sculpture that (a) does not exist, and (b) does not also exist outside of that particular painting or sculpture. Writing to his brother Theo, from the tormented exile in which he wandered, Vincent van Gogh explained that

> when I was in other surroundings, in the surroundings of pictures and objects of art, you know how I then had a violent passion for them, that reached the highest pitch of enthusiasm. And I do not repent it, for even now, *far from that land, I am often homesick for the land of pictures.* (*Letters*, 118)

Van Gogh puts those last words in italics: "the land of pictures" has a physical reality for him that, despite his parallel passion for books, did not and could not exist where mere words were concerned. Indeed, conscious explorer as he frequently was, van Gogh explicitly recognized this difference. Sending a sketch to his brother, he added in a postscript: "You see how in the sketch of the beach there is a blond tender effect, and in the wood there is a

more gloomy serious tone. I am glad both exist in life" (168–69).
The trouble with academic painting, he argued, was precisely that
it dealt with *"really non-existent figures. . . .* All academic figures
are constructed in the same way . . . irreproachably *faultless . . . I
should be desperate if my figures were correct . . .* I do not want
them to be academically correct" (234–36; emphasis in the original). It was reality rather than formulated, abstracted academic
principle he was after, and he knew it existed because his eyes told
him so. Like everyone else, he could see the lines and shapes with
which the world is filled. "Let us now turn to the human frame,"
declared the American sculptor Horatio Greenough, "the most
beautiful organization of earth. . . . Where is the ornament of this
frame? It is all beauty, its motion is grace, no combination of
harmony ever equaled, for expression and variety, its poised and
stately gait; its voice is music, no cunning mixture of wood and
metal ever did more than feebly imitate its tone of command or its
warble of love" (*Form and Function*, 120–21).

Such basic differences create, inevitably, differing mind-sets. It
is not accidental that, on the whole, musicians have been more
verbal than painters or sculptors. Visual artists can be inspired by
literature, but, at least as we in the West understand both literature
and visual art, no painter can set a poem, no sculptor can compose
in tandem, as it were, with a verbal text. Apart from their titles,
visual works have no correspondence with verbal ones that can
possibly compare with music's. Composers have written their own
librettos: there is no corresponding function that a visual artist
can perform for himself, for he cannot in any meaningful way
begin his work with words. And indeed, apart from whatever self-
clarifications the use of words can perhaps offer him, "What can
[the artist] say in words," as Ben Shahn demanded, "that he could
not far more skilfully present in pictorial form" (Sorell, 126)?
Musicians of course issue much the same disclaimer; the point is
that they more often take the trouble to employ words, in spite of
all their protests. That is, it is more natural to them than it is to
visual artists to *say*. Walter Sorell notes that "in spite of all
attempts at articulation and soul-searching, very few artists will
ever be able to say what the sources of their art are" (132). After a
long session in which he tried to write a sonnet, the painter Degas
complained to the poet Mallarmé, "What a profession! I've wasted

the whole day on a damned sonnet without progressing one step. Not that I have not got enough ideas! I am full of them, I have too many." And Mallarmé quietly and accurately replied, "One does not write poetry with ideas, Degas, but with words" (135). As Marc Chagall puts it, "If, in a picture, I have cut off a cow's head and put it on upside-down, or occasionally even painted the whole picture topsy turvy, I have not done so in order to make literature. I want to introduce into my picture a psychic shock, which always operates through pictorial factors, in other words to introduce a fourth dimension" (143). That champion of the new, Clement Greenberg, defended abstract visual art, almost half a century ago, in this revealing language:

> With the arrival of outrightly abstract art, it seemed that the picture was deprived of real space and real objects as a model for its own articulation and unity; that henceforth the norms of the medium alone would have to suffice. And in a sense, this has been the case. But in another sense—a sense far less immediately evident—it has not. Western painting has continued somehow to be naturalistic despite all appearances to the contrary. When Braque and Picasso stopped trying to imitate the normal appearance of a wineglass and tried instead to approximate, by *analogy*, the way nature opposed verticals in general to horizontals in general—at this point, [visual] art caught up with a new conception and feeling of reality that was already emerging in general sensibility as well as in science. (*Art and Culture*, 172)

In short, Braque and Picasso could not had they wanted to escape from the physical reality, the immediate and unavoidably palpable physical existence, of the materials with which they worked. No writer, no composer, is thus plunged willy-nilly into a relatively objective world that exists as much outside as inside him.

This is of course not to demand of visual art any sort of exact correspondence to everyday reality; it is certainly not to define art as in any mechanical sense representational. Rather, it should help us to understand why, even more than the musician or the literary worker, the visual artist is inescapably an organizer, a shaper as much as (in the old sense) a maker. (A "maker" once meant an "artist," and in Scotland specifically a "poet.") This is hardly a new realization. More than a century ago, Horatio Greenough roundly declared that "in art, as in nature, the soul, the purpose of a work will never fail to be proclaimed in that work in proportion to the subordination of the parts to the whole, [and] of the whole to the function" (121). No poet, no novelist, no composer would I suspect make such a statement. One might think that since literature and music are both created across time, and thus exist only in what we might call "continuities," structure would be even more important for them than it is in visual art, which plainly does not have the same constantly moving, shifting linear basis. But the truth would seem to be that, precisely because of the exigencies of controlling time as well as the other aspects of their genres, controlling structure is far more difficult in literature and music. Importance *is*, in other words, as importance *does*. The painter or sculptor has the power to far more fully control structure, and so, inevitably, that is exactly what he does. And this is really just another way of defining "importance," for the visual artist *must* control structure, because it is so basic a component of what he works with. His visual presentation has no choice but to be complete as it presents itself—and, just as pressingly, his presentation must compete, in the beholder's eye, with many, many other presentations, only a small percentage of them in any sense artistic. The viewer of paintings or sculpture does not possess, simply by virtue of his humanity, a trained eye. Hardly! But since the materials with which the visual artist works preexist in profusion, all across the many assorted landscapes that the viewer has necessarily experienced, that viewer comes to the work of visual art with an inevitable set of experientially derived touchstones. Granted, this vastly simplifies certain aspects of the visual artist's job. But it also intensifies much of the struggle that he must undertake in order to convince the viewer of the authenticity, not to say the power, of his own vision. Whatever his other troubles, neither the literary nor the musical artist has quite this obstacle to overcome. To be compared to Shakespeare, or perhaps to the Beatles, is difficult enough. To be compared to all of your audience's prior visual experience is surely infinitely harder.

Over the past century, in particular, it has become increasingly difficult for the visual artist to make that case for his art. Roger Fry's complaint, sixty years ago, could have been written for tomorrow morning's paper:

> Ordinary people have almost no idea of what things really look like, so that oddly enough the one standard that popular criticism applies to painting, namely, whether it is like nature or not, is one which most people are, by the whole tenor of their lives, prevented from applying properly. The only things they have ever really *looked* at being other pictures, the moment an artist who has looked at nature brings to them a clear report of something definitely seen by him, they are wildly indignant at its untruth to nature. (*Vision and Design*, 25)

As a very young man, totally ignorant of the changes wrought by twentieth-century painters and sculptors, I was brought to the Museum of Modern Art, in New York City—and just half an hour later, I was brought (I might better say "led") back out again, so visually confused that I was dizzy and sick to my stomach. I can still recall sitting at the edge of the curb, my feet in the street, my head in my hands, trying to rebalance the world. When I was able to stand and walk, I took a determined vow not to return until I knew what on earth was going on, after which I enrolled myself as an art student. Six months later, after rigorous study, I made my second visit—and did not recognize the place. The literally sickening paintings and sculpture had become fascinatingly beautiful explorations. I could not myself turn out such work: again, that is hardly the point. But I had begun to understand what Picasso and Braque and the others were doing; their vision of the world had become readily accessible to me. I could to some extent see as they saw, so that what my eyes now knew and could therefore experientially verify was compatible with what their eyes had seen.

I would be more troubled about such discrepancies were I not aware of the stony lack of comprehension, even the ignorant fury, with which artistic change is often met. Manet's frolicsome "Le Déjeuner sur l'herbe," exhibited in 1863, strikes us, today, as a gently erotic and quite lovely portrait of urban mores: two metropolitan cavaliers and their mistresses living the sporting life on a gay expedition into the countryside. But a typical contemporary criticism declared:

> A commonplace woman of the demimonde, as naked as can be, shamelessly lolls between two dandies dressed to the teeth. These latter look like schoolboys on a holiday, perpetrating an outrage to play the man. . . . This is a young man's practical joke, a shameful open sore not worth exhibiting. . . . The landscape is well handled . . . , but the figures are slipshod. (Hamilton, 45)

A more thoughtful but still uncomprehending critic wrote (and in this perplexed analysis we can clearly observe, very sharply and honestly exposed, the conflict between old and new ways of seeing):

> [These] are good sketches, I will grant you. There is a certain verve in the colors, a certain freedom of touch which are in no way commonplace. But then what? Is this drawing? Manet thinks himself resolute and powerful. He is only hard. And the amazing thing is that he is as soft as he is hard. That's because he is uncertain about some things and leaves them to chance. Not one detail has attained its exact and final form. I see garments without feeling the anatomical structure which supports them and explains their movements. I see boneless fingers and heads without skulls. I see side whiskers made of two strips of black cloth that could have been glued to their cheeks. What else do I see? The artist's lack of conviction and sincerity. (47–48)

Fifty years earlier, in fact, Eugène Delacroix had had to confront very similar accusations that his brilliant (and brilliantly thought out) canvases were nothing but "sketches" (*Readings in Art History*, vol. II, 259). But then, a Viennese music critic wrote, in 1804, that Beethoven's strong and lyrical Second Symphony was "a crass monster, a hideously writhing wounded dragon, that refuses to expire, and though bleeding in the Finale, furiously beats about with its tail erect" (Slonimsky, 42). Two years later, in the same city, a critic declared of Beethoven's opera, *Fidelio*, "that never was anything as incoherent, shrill, chaotic and ear-splitting produced in music. The most piercing dissonances clash in a really atrocious harmony, and a few puny ideas only increase the disagreeable and deafening effect" (Ibid.).

Let us construct a hypothetical case. An experienced, professionally active painter named Alpha is taking a walk, sketchpad tucked under his arm. He does not intend to draw anything, but like the writer who sleeps with a notebook and pencil by his side he is taking no chances. If something presents itself, either something he sees or else conjures up in his mind, he wants to be able to preserve it for later development. He is, in short, a dedicated artist, alert, fully functioning.

Not too far distant, an experienced, professionally active musician named Beta is also taking a walk. He too carries with him a notebook, though instead of blank pages it bears preprinted staves.

And just over the next hill, let us promenade an experienced, professionally active poet named Gamma, carrying a notebook ruled in standard horizontal lines.

Let us further suppose an unusually vivid and absorbing scene, something well calculated to draw the attention and stir the imagination of our three perambulating professionals. It does not matter exactly what sort of scene, but we will do better to particularize, so let us say they all three converge—each totally unaware of the other—upon a singularly beautiful, high waterfall, splashing down over a great rocky cliff. All three are immediately struck; they stop, they stare, and as their senses quicken their trained faculties start to work.

Can we characterize essentially how each of them operates? Let us proceed in reverse order, starting with Gamma, the poet.

His medium is words, so his mind tosses up a key phrase, compelling either for its mood, its metaphor, or even its rhythm. There is likely to be no structure in his mind (though he of course knows a good deal about creating verbal structures, and what particular sorts of structures are most likely, in his professional practice, to fit with the extensions and elaborations of that first phrase, already welling up and shaping themselves). He may make the first phrase the first words of whatever poem he is groping toward; he may place it later, and start to create the preparatory lines that can lead to and justify the first phrase; he may tentatively place it at the very end, and try to trace his way back to a proper starting point. By the time he has drafted the poem even in its early form, that first phrase may or may not still be in it. In my experience, the odds favor its retention, but one cannot be sure, for successive elaborations and gropings may shift mood, metaphor, and rhythm alike. If the poem remains inchoate, all the verbal clusters he has begun to shape (and perhaps has started to write down) will remain essentially shapeless: it is only when the poem has some rough existence that it also begins to acquire a more or less decisive structure. (I am avoiding the word "form," which would be applicable to poets working in what we think of as formal structures, but not applicable to poets each of whose poems must find its own organization and shape.) If the initially unformed impulse grows into some connected, meaningful order (a process that can take days, months, even years), the demands of structure become more urgent. There are poems that quickly and powerfully seem to shape themselves. They tend to be the exception. Most poems require repeated reshaping, often a long process of pruning and adding, rephrasing, filling in gaps that need elaboration and eliminating gaps that should never have been there in the first place. Phrases and lines are silently whispered in the mind (and sometimes muttered or recited aloud, especially by such peripatetic poets as our friend Gamma). Images are floated up and shot down.

Our musician, Beta, does not work with words but with pitches and their intervals, their rhythms, their speed, their dynamics. Our poet might have started, for example, by analogizing the swiftly dropping waterfall to a suddenly quenched passion, or to a moment of helpless, tumbling terror, or to the startling sense of rapid, perhaps ungovernable change. Each such metaphor obviously contains its own mood, and each mood dictates its own rhythm, and these factors must combine and unroll together for Gamma's poem to come into being. But Beta has to *hear* his work. Neither verbal nor metaphoric, it has to open itself to him as a possibility of linear sequence, sometimes with specific colorations already attached. There is, again, not likely to be any initial awareness of structure: in a sense, Beta too starts with a phrase, though of a different sort. But as his linear sequences extend and grow longer, more complex, organization and structure necessarily start to be imposed at a much earlier point. The poet can go for a very long time, in the process of verbal composition, without imposing order. The musician cannot, precisely because of the inherent linearity of his materials. Without an early sense of order, those sequences dribble away and become meaningless. And as Beta imagines fuller and richer sequences, he inevitably starts also to hear the dynamic ranges through which those sequences must move. As he starts to hear the contrapuntal aspects of his work, he creates accompanying time changes, assorted voices (that is, musical lines), each weaving its particular web. As he fills in (or "realizes") harmony, the sheer density and complexity of his music absolutely requires of him that he build in terms of the structure or structures he has imagined. What Igor Stravinsky planned as a piano concerto mutated into the ballet *Petrouchka*—but the underlying structure did not have to change anything like as much as our poet, Gamma, would have had to change *his* work had it become, say, an epic poem or a television script. If the musical shapes are small enough, to be sure, they can be made to fit into a variety of larger structures. Not many poets can work that way, though T. S. Eliot frequently did, often publishing the parts of a poem in helter-skelter order and only at the very end establishing its final shape. But then, Eliot is also the only major poet in any language or literature known to me ever to publish a major poem, "The Waste Land," that did not take its final shape from his hand but instead from that of his friend and advisor, Ezra Pound.

And Alpha, our visual artist? He virtually begins by creating the structure his work will have. He not only employs preexisting shapes, but he also works within a predetermined space, the boundaries of which are the paper or canvas on which he draws. And if at first he produces only fragments of a larger work (i.e., if he produces what are called "studies"), when he comes to the point that the larger work finally incorporates these studies, he necessarily adapts them to its structure, changing as he needs to their size, their tonality, and so on. Alpha does not see the waterfall and the cliff as primarily metaphor or symbolization, but rather as a visually provocative assemblage of shapes and lines and colors. Nor does he think in terms of sequences (unless of course he turns out a series of interconnected works, such a series being the only way in which he can attain to the musician's inevitable sense of movement in time). Whether he is a representational or a nonrepresentational artist is a great deal less important than the decisions he starts to make about weight and mass, about tonality, about light and dark. The poet thinks in words, the musician thinks in sounds, but in essence the visual artist thinks with his brain at the end of his arm. (I pretty much exclude conceptual art from these remarks, because its fundamental assumptions seem to me largely to differentiate it from what I am tempted to call true visual art. I am quite prepared to be called old-fashioned or even prejudiced; I am also prepared to defend these positions, as I have done many times before, both publicly and privately.) "Color is as intimate to her as the musical note that passes through the ear to innermost organs of sense," as one critic wrote of the painter Georgia O'Keeffe. O'Keeffe's biographer, Laurie Lisle, adds:

> She thought in color the way others . . . thought in words.
> . . . Despite the fact that she had a strong, vivid, and distinctive writing style, she said that words were often false, meaningless, and limited. Pigment, on the other hand, was trustworthy. . . . "I see no reason for painting anything that can be put into any other form as well," she once said, explaining that she preferred to paint her feeling about something rather than talk about it. She used to tell frustrated interviewers that she didn't like to think in words, that words were "inelastic." (279–80)

Significantly, many sculptors have explained that they see their task as releasing a certain form from the material in which they find it confined. The structure, that is, is for them not only concurrent with their work but actually preexistent. Sculpture, being three-dimensional, is of course decidedly more structural in its nature than painting or drawing. But the principle is nicely illustrative, all the same. And the very extravagances of Enrico Prampolini's 1913 Futurist manifesto are based on visual art's close, enduring connections with visual reality:

> If we conceive of painting as an aggregation of chromatic vibrations we should remember that the principles on

which future painting must be established will be those of pure atmospheric visibility. The aim will be to encourage the optical appreciation of fine distinctions, atmospheric subtleties, and rhythmic influences of the atom, and to be able to express in chromatic terms the sound waves and the vibrations of all movements within the atmosphere. (*Futurist Manifestos*, 115)

I do not mean to suggest that visual art is any less interpretative, and thus less meaningful, or less closely tied to other aspects of human existence, than are the other arts. Our friend Alpha may proceed differently, in conceiving and then in executing his paintings and drawings, but in the end—exactly like Beta and Gamma— his work deals with the same fundamental human issues. It should not have been too hard, listening to my brief description of the three men's modus operandi, to change a word here and a word there and come up with a description applicable to social science, science, and indeed to virtually any human activity calling for sensitivity to both thought and emotion. It may help to cite, here, Arnold Hauser's fine exposition of the late nineteenth-century movement known as Impressionism. Note in particular how deftly, and also how accurately, Hauser connects this way of approaching visual art to other basic human concerns. Again, change a word here and a word there and Hauser might well be talking about economics or history, about science and technology, or about literature and music:

Impressionism is an urban art, and not only because it discovers the landscape quality of the city and brings painting back from the country into the town, but because it sees the world through the eyes of the townsman and reacts to external impressions with the overstrained nerves of the modern technical man. It is an urban style, because it describes the changeability, the nervous rhythm, the sudden, sharp but always ephemeral impressions of city life. And precisely as such, it implies an enormous expansion of sensual perception, a new sharpening of sensibility, a new irritability, and, with the Gothic and romanticism, it signifies one of the most important turning points in the

history of Western art. In the dialectical process repre-
sented by the history of painting, the alternation of the
static and the dynamic, of design and color, abstract order
and organic life, impressionism forms the climax of the
development in which recognition is given to the dynamic
and organic elements of experience and which completely
dissolves the static world-view of the Middle Ages. A
continuous line can be traced from the Gothic to impressionism, comparable to the line leading from late medieval
economy to high capitalism. . . . (*The Social History of
Art*, IV, 168)

And operating from a very different perspective—his goal being
the linkages between art and religion and philosophy—Wilhelm
Worringer makes an almost identical point:

The banal theories of imitation, which our aesthetics has
never shaken off, . . . have blinded us to the true psychic
values which are the point of departure and the goal of all
artistic creation. . . . All artistic creation is nothing less
than a continual registration of the great process of disputation, in which man and the outer world have been
engaged, and will be engaged, from the dawn of creation
until the end of time. Thus art is simply one more form for
the expression of those psychic energies which, anchored
in the same process, determine the phenomenon of religion
and of changing world views. . . . [This] process of disputation between man and the outer world naturally takes
place solely within man, and is in truth nothing else than a
disputation between instinct and understanding. (*Abstraction and Empathy*, 127–29)

The anthropologist John L. Fischer seems to me to be arguing,
once again, exactly the same point, except from neither a social-
cultural nor a religious-philosophic, but from a psychoanalytic
perspective. "In expressive aspects of culture," he says,

such as visual and other arts, a very important determinant
of the art form is social fantasy, that is, the artist's fantasies

about social situations which will give him security or pleasure. . . . Regardless of the overt content of visual art, whether a landscape, a natural object, or merely a geometrical pattern, there is always or nearly always at the same time the expression of some fantasied social situation which will bear a definite relation to the real and desired social situations of the artist and his society. (*Anthropology and Art*, 142–43)

Fischer's argument, indeed, brings us right back to the main theme of this book, namely, that what we choose to call artistic creativity is nothing more or less than the heightened engagement of human beings with themselves, their fellows, and their environment. What Fischer, Worringer, and Hauser have said about visual art could—and in my judgment *should*—be said not only about art, but about every aspect of human concern. And I would go somewhat further than Fischer, who cautiously notes that "there is always *or nearly always*" a link between what an artist produces and his stance toward his own and his society's place and posture in the world. I reject his caution and would strike the words "or nearly always." I do not think it is possible for *any* human being to escape these linkages. The artist is neither better nor worse than his fellow human beings, only somewhat different, somewhat more aware of and in harmony with certain aspects of our common existence and, more than likely, somewhat less aware of and in tune with others. A singularly wealthy self-made man with whom I worked, not too long ago, used to say seriously, albeit with a smile, that he suspected he could make untold millions if he outlined proposed business deals to me, listened carefully to my advice, and then proceeded to do exactly the opposite of whatever I suggested. "You have," he assured me, "less business sense than any man I have ever met." He was right, and though I do not desire business sense, having more than enough other matters to occupy me, I would be a pretentious fool if I maintained that my deficiency in these areas was anything but a deficiency. Where would the world be if everyone had my degree of concern for business and monetary affairs? But, fortunately, we do not need to worry. The world is an immensely varied place, with room to spare for all sorts of talents, working in all sorts of directions. And that fact, in turn, also stands right at the base of my entire argument through-out this book. Just as we recognize and even celebrate the incredible variability of the world and of all the human beings in it, so too we must learn to recognize, and try to exploit to the fullest, the large possibilities that can come from teaching ourselves (or should I say *freeing* ourselves?) to use in our own lives the creative tools employed by the artist. We know that we do not need to be musicians to enjoy Beethoven, or the Beatles. Why don't we understand that, fundamentally, what drives and empowers Beethoven is no different from what can drive and empower each and all of us, whatever our area of professional concern? We only fool ourselves if we neglect and even close off those centers of force and possibility. We are all, like it or not, intuitive and illogical, irrational and emotional, quite as much as (and perhaps even more than) we are trained and logical, rational and dispassionate. There is no such thing as rational man, there is no such thing as dispassionate man. There is only the same old human being we have all always been, trying foolishly and sometimes dangerously to trick himself and his fellows into believing that he, uniquely, has transcended basic human nature. But no merely human being transcends humanity—and the best, the most fully human of human beings, are those of us who strive constantly and unceasingly to be the most intensely human we can be.

Which brings me, finally, to the necessity for making some concrete, and I hope practical, recommendations. Analysis is essential, but analysis that does not lead to implementation tends to be arid.

I speak from and to the university community, but if there is any validity to the observations I have been making in this book, then most of what I have to say should be applicable beyond that important yet limited small world.

How do we put ourselves in touch with our creative centers? And how do we break down the artificial and severely restricting barriers between professions and bodies of knowledge? First, and perhaps primarily, we allow ourselves to experience the new and the different. Regularly and even systematically, we give ourselves the opportunity to stretch to fit new and different ways of seeing and understanding. These are neither abstract nor terribly difficult injunctions, though they do require of us persistence and determination. Books and journals and articles in fields other than our own often seem unattractive, not to say impenetrable—and where do we find the time, even if we teem with desire? The old maxim applies: if you want something done, ask a busy man. Time can always be found. We are not so gridlocked into our busy schedules that we cannot manage, say, one book a month outside our own fields. Nor does venturesomeness require of us stupidity. I am perfectly aware, for example, that for me to tackle a professional journal in physical chemistry, or microbiology, would be to waste rather than to improve time. Even the essays on those subjects in a more or less general-purpose magazine like *Scientific American* are forbidding. (I have been gratified to hear from good practicing scientists that they too regularly have trouble understanding essays in that magazine, outside their own fields.) But I have found that, struggling catch-as-catch-can with such essays, I somehow manage to pick up something, each time, that enables me to understand and acquire something else when next I tackle a similar essay. And material from all one's reading constantly feeds into and informs these struggles. Again, a professor of humanities like myself is not called upon to teach quantum mechanics or microbial cell structure. But to understand such matters does help me, daily, to make sense of a dozen more narrowly defined texts that *are* my primary responsibility. This is of course an inevitable process, given the absolutely unavoidable unity of human experience.

Reading is to be sure not our only way of acquiring knowledge and information. Listening comes into play, too—and not simply listening to ourselves. Professors sometimes have a habit of limiting their listening to the sounds that emerge from their own mouths. It helps to listen to others, even other professors, and especially other professors whose training and experience are in different vineyards. One of the best academic innovations I know of was created by the experimental psychologist Kenneth Purcell, when he was functioning as dean of the College of Arts and Sciences at the University of Denver. Seven or eight times each academic year, Ken supplied a comfortable meeting place and a simple sandwich lunch to any member of the faculty who wanted to attend an after-lunch talk on the recent research activity of another member of the faculty. A not-overburdened faculty committee handled all the arrangements; Ken's office paid the exceedingly modest bills.

Scientists, musicians, historians, teachers of literature, and more regularly attended, and just as regularly had their minds opened and stretched, not least by the question-and-answer periods that followed each such presentation. All universities have departmental symposia. Why do they not all have interdepartmental symposia? I regularly submit my own work, including the drafts of the lectures that became this book, to people whose judgment I respect—and among the most useful comments I receive are those that come from a brilliantly interdisciplinary psychiatric sociologist and a superb hands-on editor who works with computer education at a major industrial-consulting firm. I listen to professors of English, too; I also listen to my wife, who happens to be a fine and well-published writer. To be perfectly blunt, I am always prepared to listen to anybody and everybody who may have anything sensible to say. A total stranger once walked up to me at a convention and, after saying (and being thanked for saying) that he liked my translations from the Old English, asked why I had translated a particular expression as I had, instead of in a different way. I made a note, thought about the comment, and in the next printing changed the translation. Why not? He was right, and I was, if not wrong, at least not as right. Why not be as right as you can, since none of us can ever possibly be perfect?

We need to listen to more than words. Music is singularly compelling to me. It may not produce the same effect on you. But have you given it a fair chance, have you given yourself a fair chance? I was over thirty, and had been listening to classical music for fifteen years, before I could tolerate the music of the twentieth century. But I kept trying, and finally a door was opened, a massive, titanic door, through which enormous profit and pleasure have poured. Because I began my abortive musical career wishing to be a New Orleans jazz clarinetist—Johnny Dodds was my idol, but I would have settled for playing like George Lewis; by now I think I would settle for playing like either Steve or Woody Allen—it was hard, very hard, for me to understand or like John Coltrane and Ornette Coleman and Miles Davis. I kept listening, and at just about my fiftieth birthday I began to understand, I began to appreciate. It's never too late: that too is obviously another moral we need to keep in mind.

Universities are delighted to take money from private industry.

If indeed a successful businessman understands some things that we do not, why don't we also take *ideas* from him? How many corporate executives have been invited to address academic symposia? How many departments and colleges have recognized that at these levels, too, experience from outside the academic world can be useful and have therefore sought ways to incorporate (the word itself is surely significant) that experience into their own governing structures? We have outside chairmen on our doctoral-defense committees. Would we gain or lose from having outside members on other departmental and collegewide committees? Would not our understanding of the communities within which we work, and that we seek in many other ways to make aware of our mission and our accomplishments, be powerfully strengthened by such interactions? And would not community understanding, and perhaps ultimately community support, be strengthened as well? Are we in the university world either so immeasurably superior, or so much weaker-minded, that a single outside voice on a departmental or a collegewide committee could traduce our mission, betray our independence, and seduce our faculty?

We have students on some of our departmental committees. Why don't we also have students who are no longer students? I refer, of course, to alumni. Why is homecoming week the only time when former students are asked to involve themselves in any way with a university that can enrich itself with their brains as well as their checkbooks?

I taught my first university class more than forty years ago; I have served on more departmental committees than I could possibly enumerate. Why have I never seen an English department curriculum committee that included professors from other departments that also deal with literature—other departments that serve much the same student clientele; other departments that include bright, well-trained people whose interests and training and daily work are much the same; other departments, last but definitely not least, that coexist *in the same university*? It is not enough for departments to be polite and even cooperative with one another; it is certainly disastrous for departments to see themselves (and alas, as you know, they often do see themselves) as intrinsically hostile to and competitive with one another. Why cannot departments truly *work* together, sharing faculty as well as ideas and experience and students? There are practical obstacles: I am well aware of some of them, having served for a time as a dean. But these are surely overcomable obstacles, if we truly want to overcome them—and in such a cause, how can we not want to overcome them?

Creativity is not some special milk of human genius, available only to a select few. It is our common birthright, available to all of us, although in different degrees and to be sure in different ways. We are too much concerned with genius and too little concerned with ourselves. Neither the poet nor the great poet nor the toweringly great poet are intrinsically any better than the man who hauls away our trash or the man who dispenses medicine to our children. Nor are they intrinsically any different, except that they happen to write poetry, or great poetry, or toweringly great poetry. We can and must make distinctions between and among trash haulers and medicine dispensers, some of whom do their work better than others, and some of whom do their work supremely well. Honor to the best among trash haulers, and to the best among medicine dispensers, and honor, also, to the best among poets. I do not argue for a leveling among those who follow any of life's pathways. All poets are no more created equal than are all trash haulers or all medicine dispensers. I am, as I understand the term, a fierce elitist. But I completely fail to see why poetry or the practice of any other art is intrinsically any different, or any better, than hauling trash or dispensing medicine. The arts are certainly not any worse, but they are simply another way in which the variety of the human spirit and the human necessity manifest themselves. We would be woefully badly off if our trash were not hauled away as efficiently as possible; our children, and thus we ourselves, would be very badly off if proper medicines were not intelligently dispensed. It would be a disaster for our country, our world, and all of humankind still to come if poetry, and great poetry, and toweringly great poetry were not being produced. Someone has to do the best job possible of hauling away the trash, someone has to do the best job possible of dispensing medicines, and someone has to write the best possible poetry. All occupations are honorable, per se, if honorably performed. No one deserves special commendation simply for doing what he has to do, though he may well deserve blame for how badly or commendation for how well he does it. And every trash hauler, every dispenser of medicine, and every poet can learn to do their jobs still better, can find and invent ways, if they want to, to perform more effectively.

So it is not "geniuses" about whom I have been talking. I don't like either the word or the concept that frames it, as I also intensely dislike hero worship and all forms of personal adulation. Respect the act, not the actor. Respect the worth of what has been done, not he who does it. Stand on your own hind legs and recognize, for it is true, that you are intrinsically as good a man, or a woman, as any so-called genius. You may not be able to haul trash as well; you may not be able to dispense medicine as well; you may not be able to write poetry as well. But there are things in your life you can do, things you do do, as well and quite possibly as superlatively as Albert Einstein or T. S. Eliot did what they did.

And what you do not yet do well, you can learn to do well. No man or woman of normal endowment has ever appeared on this earth empty of that potential. There is every bit as much creativity in you—or, more accurately, there can be, if you will let it. Your constant task, and mine, is to encourage ourselves to fulfill that potential. Honor the accomplishments of others only if you also honor your own. This is hardly a new rule, let me remind you, but one that was laid down four thousand and more years ago: "Thou shalt not make unto thee any graven image, or any likeness of any thing that is in heaven above, or that is in the earth beneath, or that is in the water under the earth: Thou shalt not bow down thyself to them, nor serve them" (Exodus 20:4–5). No man, living or dead, should be turned into a graven image. And all men living should strive to be, as they were meant to be, as much themselves as over the years of their lives they can manage to become. No one can ask more of you than that. But neither should anyone ask less, either of himself or of anyone else.

WORKS CITED

[Adams, Henry] *Letters of Henry Adams, 1858–1891*, ed. Worthington Chauncey Ford (Boston: Houghton Mifflin, 1930).

[Adams, Henry] *Letters of Henry Adams, 1892–1918*, ed. Worthington Chauncey Ford (Boston: Houghton Mifflin, 1938).

Anthropology and Art: Readings in Cross-Cultural Aesthetics, ed. Charlotte M. Otten (Garden City, N.Y.: Natural History Press, 1971).

Artists as Professors: see under Risenhoover, Morris.

Asimov, Isaac, *Asimov's Biographical Encyclopedia of Science and Technology*, 2d ed., rev. (Garden City, N.Y.: Doubleday, 1982).

Bakan, David, *Sigmund Freud and the Jewish Mystical Tradition* (Princeton, N.J.: Van Nostrand, 1958; reprint ed., New York: Schocken, 1965).

Becker, Carl, *Detachment and the Writing of History* (Ithaca, N.Y.: Cornell University Press, 1958).

Bell, Daniel, *The Cultural Contradictions of Capitalism* (New York: Basic, 1976).

[Berlioz, Hector] *The Memoirs of Hector Berlioz* (London: Gollancz, 1969; reprint ed., London: Panther, 1970).

Bernstein, Leonard, *The Joy of Music* (New York: Simon and Schuster, 1959).

Bloch, Marc, *The Historian's Craft* (New York: Knopf, 1953; reprint ed., New York: Vintage, n.d.).

Bronowski, Jacob, *Science and Human Values*, rev. ed. (New York: Harper, 1965).

Butterfield, Herbert, *The Origins of Modern Science, 1300–1800*, rev. ed. (London: Bell, 1957; reprint ed., New York: Collier, 1962).

[Carter, Elliott] Allen Edwards, *Flawed Words and Stubborn Sounds: A Conversation with Elliott Carter* (New York: Norton, 1971).

Cary, Joyce, *Art and Reality: Ways of the Creative Process* (New York: Harper, 1958; reprint ed., Garden City, N.Y.: Doubleday, 1961).

Cary, Joyce, *Selected Essays*, ed. A. G. Bishop (New York: St. Martin's, 1976).

Castelnuovo-Tedesco, Mario, "Problems of a Song-Writer," in *Reflections on Art: A Source Book of Writings by Artists, Critics, and Philosophers*, ed. Susanne K. Langer (Baltimore, Md.: Johns Hopkins University Press, 1958; reprint ed., New York: Oxford University Press, 1961).

Chandrasekhar, S., *Truth and Beauty: Aesthetics and Motivations in Science* (Chicago: University of Chicago Press, 1987).

[Conrad, Joseph] *Letters from Joseph Conrad*, ed. Edward Garnett (Indianapolis, Ind.: Bobbs-Merrill, 1928; reprint ed., Indianapolis, Ind.: Charter, 1962).

Cooke, Deryck, *The Language of Music* (New York: Oxford University Press, 1959).

Copland, Aaron, *Music and Imagination* (Cambridge, Mass.: Harvard University Press, 1952; reprint ed., New York: Mentor, 1959).

Darwin, Charles, *Autobiography* (London: Watts, 1929).

[Debussy, Claude] *Prelude to "The Afternoon of a Faun": An Authoritative Score*, ed. William W. Austin (New York: Norton, 1970).

[Dos Passos, John] *The Fourteenth Chronicle: Letters and Diaries of John Dos Passos* (Boston: Gambit, 1973).

Edelman, Gerald M., *Neural Darwinism: The Theory of Neuronal Group Selection* (New York: Basic, 1987).

Eisenstadt, A. Sidney, ed., *The Craft of American History*, 2 vols. (New York: Harper, 1966).

Ellmann, Richard, *James Joyce*, rev. ed. (New York: Oxford University Press, 1982; reprint ed., corrected, New York: Oxford University Press, 1983).

Erickson, Robert, *The Structure of Music* (New York: Noonday, 1955).

Evans, Ifor, *Literature and Science* (London: Allen and Unwin, 1954).

Feuer, Lewis S., *The Scientific Intellectual: The Psychological and Sociological Origins of Modern Science* (New York: Basic, 1963).

FitzGerald, Frances, *America Revised: History Schoolbooks in the Twentieth Century* (Boston: Little Brown, 1979).

Freud, Sigmund, *Civilization and Its Discontents*, trans. James Strachey (New York: Norton, 1962).

Freud, Sigmund, *The Origins of Psychoanalysis: Letters, Drafts and Notes to Wilhelm Fliess, 1887–1902* (New York: Basic, 1954; reprint ed., New York: Anchor, 1957).

Fry, Roger, *Vision and Design* (London: Chatto and Windus, 1920; reprint ed., New York: Meridian, 1956).

Futurist Manifestos, ed. Umbro Apollonio (New York: Viking, 1973).

Ghiselin, Brewster, ed., *The Creative Process* (Berkeley: University of California Press; reprint ed., New York: Mentor, 1955).

[Gide, André] *The Journals of André Gide*, ed. Justin O'Brien, 2 vols. (New York: Knopf, 1947–51; reprint ed., New York: Vintage, 1956).

Ginsberg, Allen, *Allen Verbatim: Lectures on Poetry, Politics, Consciousness*, ed. Gordon Ball (New York: McGraw-Hill, 1974).

Gleick, James, *Chaos* (New York: Viking, 1987).
Goldstein, Martin, and Inge F. Goldstein, *How We Know: An Exploration of the Scientific Process* (New York: Plenum, 1978).
Greenberg, Clement, *Art and Culture* (Boston: Beacon, 1961).
Greenough, Horatio, *Form and Function*, ed. Harold A. Small (Berkeley: University of California Press, 1947).
Hamilton, George Heard, *Manet and His Critics* (New Haven, Conn.: Yale University Press, 1954; reprint ed., New York: Norton, 1969).
Hauser, Arnold, *The Social History of Art*, 4 vols. (New York: Vintage, 1958).
Higham, John, ed., *The Reconstruction of American History* (London: Hutchinson, 1962; reprint ed., New York: Harper, 1962).
Hindemith, Paul, *A Composer's World* (Cambridge, Mass.: Harvard University Press, 1952; reprint ed., Garden City, N.Y.: Doubleday, 1961).
Housman, A. E., *Selected Prose*, ed. John Carter (Cambridge: Cambridge University Press, 1962).
Hughes, H. Stuart, *The Sea Change: The Migration of Social Thought, 1930–1965* (New York: Harper, 1975).
Huxley, Aldous, *Collected Essays* (New York: Bantam, 1960).
Irvine, William, *Apes, Angels, and Victorians: Darwin, Huxley, and Evolution* (New York: McGraw-Hill, 1955; reprint ed., New York: Meridian, 1959).
Jaynes, Julian, *The Origin of Consciousness in the Breakdown of the Bicameral Mind* (Boston: Houghton Mifflin, 1976).
Keller, Evelyn Fox, *A Feeling for the Organism: The Life and Work of Barbara McClintock* (New York: Freeman, 1983).
Kline, Morris, *Mathematics in Western Culture* (London: Scientific Book Guild, 1954).
Kolodin, Irving, ed., *The Composer as Listener* (New York: Horizon, 1958; reprint ed., New York: Collier, 1962).
Kuhn, Thomas S., *The Structure of Scientific Revolutions*, 2d ed. (Chicago: University of Chicago Press, 1970).
Langer, Susanne K., "The Cultural Importance of Art," in *Philosophical Sketches* (Baltimore, Md.: Johns Hopkins University Press, 1962; reprint ed., New York: Mentor, 1964).
Langer, Susanne K., *Feeling and Form: A Theory of Art* (New York: Scribner's, 1953).
Lawrence, D. H., *Phoenix: The Posthumous Papers of D. H. Lawrence*, ed. Edward D. McDonald (London: Heinemann, 1936).
Lawrence, D. H., *Psychoanalysis and the Unconscious* and *Fantasia of the Unconscious* (New York: Seltzer, 1921 and 1922; reprint ed., New York: Viking, 1960).
Lisle, Laurie, *Portrait of an Artist: A Biography of Georgia O'Keeffe* (New York: Seaview, 1980).
McClintock, Barbara: see under Keller, Evelyn Fox.
Mann, Thomas, *Letters of Thomas Mann, 1889–1955* (New York: Knopf, 1971).
Margenau, Henry, and J. E. Smith, "Philosophy of Physical Science in the Twentieth Century," in *The Evolution of Science*, ed. Guy S. Metraux and Francois Crouzet (New York: Mentor, 1963).
Mellers, Wilfrid, *Music in the Making* (London: Dobson, 1952).
Mellers, Wilfrid, *Twilight of the Gods: The Beatles in Retrospect* (London: Faber, 1973).

[Mencken, Henry L.] *Letters of H. L. Mencken*, ed. Guy J. Forgue (New York: Knopf, 1961; reprint ed., Boston: Northeastern University Press, 1981).

Miller, Arthur I., *Imagery in Scientific Thought: Creating Twentieth-Century Physics* (Boston: Birkhaeuser, 1984).

Miller, Walter M., Jr., *A Canticle for Leibowitz* (Philadelphia: Lippincott, 1960).

[Mozart, Wolfgang Amadeus] *Mozart's Letters*, ed. Eric Blom (Harmondsworth: Penguin, 1956).

Neff, Emery, *The Poetry of History* (New York: Columbia University Press, 1947).

Nisbet, Robert, *Sociology as an Art Form* (New York: Oxford University Press, 1976).

[O'Casey, Sean] *The Letters of Sean O'Casey, 1910–1941*, ed. David Krause (New York: Macmillan, 1975).

O'Keeffe, Georgia: see under Lisle, Laurie.

Orwell, George, *Selected Essays* (Harmondsworth: Penguin, 1957).

Papert, Seymour, *Mindstorms: Children, Computers, and Powerful Ideas* (New York: Basic, 1980).

Piaget, Jean, *Psychology and Epistemology* (New York: Viking, 1971).

Plumb, J. H., *The Death of the Past* (London: Macmillan, 1969; reprint ed., Harmondsworth: Penguin, 1973).

Poincaré, Henri, *Science and Hypothesis* (1902; reprint ed., New York: Dover, 1952).

Popper, Karl, *The Open Society and Its Enemies* (Princeton, N.J.: Princeton University Press, 1950).

Prawer, S. S., ed., *The Penguin Book of Lieder* (Harmondsworth: Penguin, 1964).

Raffel, Burton, *The Forked Tongue: A Study of the Translation Process* (The Hague: Mouton, 1971).

Readings in Art History, ed. Harold Spencer, rev. ed., 2 vols. (New York: Scribner's, 1976).

Riesman, David, with Nathan Glazer and Reuel Denney, *The Lonely Crowd* (New Haven, Conn.: Yale University Press, 1950; reprint ed., abridged, 1969).

Risenhoover, Morris, and Robert T. Blackburn, *Artists as Professors: Conversations with Musicians, Painters, Sculptors* (Urbana: University of Illinois Press, 1976).

Russell, Claire, and W. M. S. Russell, *Human Behavior* (Boston: Little, Brown, 1961).

Sagan, Eli, *The Lust to Annihilate: A Psychoanalytic Study of Violence in Ancient Greek Culture* (New York: Psychohistory Press, 1979).

[Sapir, Edward] *Selected Writings of Edward Sapir*, ed. D. B. Mandelbaum (Berkeley: University of California Press, 1958).

Schumann, Robert, *On Music and Musicians* (New York: Pantheon, 1946).

Seferis, George, *On the Greek Style: Selected Essays on Poetry and Hellenism*, ed. Rex Warner (London: Bodley Head, 1966).

Sessions, Roger, *The Musical Experience of Composer, Performer, Listener* (Princeton, N.J.: Princeton University Press, 1950; reprint ed., New York: Atheneum, 1962).

Shaw, George Bernard, *Collected Letters, 1898–1910*, ed. Dan H. Laurence (New York: Dodd, Mead, 1972).

Shotwell, James T., *The Story of Ancient History* (New York: Columbia University Press, 1939).

[Sibelius, Jean] Erik Tawaststjerna, *Sibelius*, vol. 1, 1865–1905 (Berkeley: University of California Press, 1976).

Slobin, Dan I., *Psycholinguistics* (Glenview, Ill.: Scott, Foresman, 1970).

Slonimsky, Nicolas, *Lexicons of Musical Invective: Critical Assaults on Composers since Beethoven's Time*, 2d ed. (Seattle: University of Washington Press, 1969).

Sorell, Walter, *The Duality of Vision: Genius and Versatility in the Arts* (Indianapolis, Ind.: Bobbs-Merrill, 1974).

Starer, Robert, *Continuo: A Life in Music* (New York: Random, 1987).

[Strauss, Richard] *A Working Friendship: The Correspondence between Richard Strauss and Hugo von Hofmannsthal* (New York: Random, 1952; reprint ed., New York: Vienna House, 1961).

Stravinsky, Igor, *An Autobiography* (New York: Simon and Schuster, 1936; reprint ed., New York: Norton, 1962).

Stravinsky, Igor, *Conversations with Robert Craft* and *Memories and Commentaries* (London: Faber, 1959, 1960; reprint ed., Harmondsworth: Penguin, 1962).

Stravinsky, Igor, *Poetics of Music, in the Form of Six Lessons* (Cambridge, Mass.: Harvard University Press, 1947; reprint ed., New York: Vintage, 1956).

Suzuki, D. T., *An Introduction to Zen Buddhism* (London: Rider, 1949; reprint ed., London: Grey Arrow, 1959).

Sypher, Wylie, *Literature and Technology* (New York: Random, 1968).

Thomson, Virgil, *Music with Words* (New Haven, Conn.: Yale University Press, 1989).

Tolkien, J. R. R., *Beowulf: The Monsters and the Critics* (London: Proceedings of the British Academy, XXII, 1937; reprint ed., London: Oxford University Press, 1958).

Turner, Frederick, *Natural Classicism: Essays on Literature and Science* (New York: Paragon, 1985).

Van Gogh, Vincent, *Letters*, ed. Mark Roskill (London: Fontana, 1963).

Waddington, C. H., *The Scientific Attitude*, 2d ed. (Harmondsworth: Penguin, 1948).

[Wagner, Richard] *Correspondence of Wagner and Liszt*, 2d ed., 2 vols. (New York: Scribner's, 1897; reprint ed., New York: Vienna House, 1973).

Watson, James D., *The Double Helix* (New York: Atheneum, 1968; reprint ed., New York: Signet, 1969).

Whorf, Benjamin L., *Language, Thought, and Reality*, ed. J. B. Carroll (Cambridge, Mass.: M.I.T. Press, 1956).

Wilson, Edward O., *Sociobiology*, abridged edition (Cambridge, Mass.: Harvard University Press, 1980).

Woolf, Virginia, *To the Lighthouse* (London: Hogarth Press, 1927; reprint ed., London: Granada, 1977).

Worringer, Wilhelm, *Abstraction and Empathy: A Contribution to the Psychology of Style* (New York: World, 1967).

[Yeats, William Butler] *The Letters of W. B. Yeats*, ed. Allan Wade (New York: Macmillan, 1955).

Zuckerkandl, Victor, *Sound and Symbol: Music and the External World* (Princeton, N.J.: Princeton University Press, 1956).

INDEX